Scottish Golf Links

Scottish Golf Links

A PHOTOGRAPHER'S JOURNEY

PHOTOGRAPHY BY IAIN MACFARLANE LOWE

HISTORICAL COMMENTARY BY DAVID JOY

ARCHITECTURAL OBSERVATIONS BY KYLE PHILLIPS

CLOCK TOWER PRESS

Clock Tower Press
3622 W. Liberty
Ann Arbor, MI 48103
www.clocktowerpress.com

For corporate or quantity gift sales, please contact our sales department: 1-800-956-8999.

Designed by Savitski Design, Ann Arbor, Michigan
Printed and bound in Singapore.

10 9 8 7 6 5 4 3 2 1

Library of Congress Cataloging-in-Publication Data on file.

ISBN: 1-932202-12-9

All inquiries for photography to
Iain M Lowe
10 Fergusson Place
St. Andrews
Fife KY16 9NF
UK
www.st-andrews-studio.co.uk

History
David Joy
www.golf-historian.co.uk

Architecture
Kyle Phillips
www.kylephillips.com

ACKNOWLEDGEMENT

Travelling the length and breadth of Scotland visiting these memorable courses in pursuit of material for this book has been an absolute joy. I have seen the sun rise and set under the most beautiful conditions that nature can contrive. I have had the pleasure of meeting golfers from around the world, travellers who daily honour these courses by their presence on them.

But none of us would have these wonderful courses to play and enjoy if it were not for the actions of those who determined to start and continue this game and, if ground was lost to erosion or man's act, move and modify. They went much further than this by setting out rules and an expectation of honesty and open friendliness that has survived, with a sense of honour, through to this day. To all of these people I bow my head in thanks for all that golf is, it's challenge, it's fellowship and it's variety.

My journey has been long and is one that I would not have accomplished without the support of my family. My parents have always been there when needed and the passing of my father in August 2003 leaves a void impossible to fill. To my wife Muriel, who has endured years of my 2am "off to a golf course" comings and goings, I promise more regularity, love and time. And finally my son Chris, who makes me as proud as any parent can be, has patiently helped with numerous tasks to ease my burden. Now is your time.

— Iain Macfarlane Lowe

ROYAL DORNOCH #4 SHADOWS EMPHASIZE THE CHALLENGE OF THE 4TH
GREEN. TO THE LEFT OF PICTURE THE 12TH AND 13TH GREENS WITH THE 14TH
"FOXY" IN THE DISTANCE.

Driven by photography, this journey around beautiful Scotland and its links courses has taken six years and over 120,000 miles to complete. It may seem a rather extended trip, but my one ambition was to allow the photography to show the courses as they are played but rarely seen. It required many visits to get the sun in just the right position and allow shadows and seasonal texture to highlight the issues that the resident golfer, with the benefit of familiarity, considers when playing a shot. I hope that this should be valuable information to the visitor as well as confirmation to all readers that the Scottish links, in my opinion, is the ultimate golfing experience.

Golf may be the main attraction for many, but there is far more depth to this country for those who wish to delve. There is the seasonal beauty of the hills and glens, Scotland's most famous wee nip and dramatic old towns and cities. To make this photographic journey complete I have, from time to time, diverted from the main path to include the variety of scenery that abounds in Scotland as well as a more modern view of its historical buildings.

Of course the history goes back many centuries and is integral to golf. But I want the text to be easy reading and not a heavy manuscript of dates and regurgitated stories. I have therefore turned to fourth generation St. Andrean and golf historian David Joy to add comment. Best known as "the man who plays Tom Morris," David's knowledge of the origins of the game and the history that spawned it is unrivalled and his text reads like a personal conversation over a drink after a good round of golf. The passion he feels for this game comes flooding through in the way he talks and writes.

The majority of these courses have evolved over many decades, indeed centuries. If they still thrill, excite and challenge the modern golfer this is in part due to their varied settings, though in many cases it is also attributable to design.

I have turned to internationally acclaimed designer Kyle Phillips from California to add some observations and diagrams covering one hole on each of the top twelve courses. It is the particular use of natural or old, manmade features as well as the relatively modern, strategic placing of bunkers that combine to offer so many risk and reward options to the golfer.

Links golf is a unique game. Undulating fairways, cavernous bunkers, blind tee or approach shots, tight lies, a hard playing surface and of course the vagaries of the ever-changeable Scottish coastal weather all make this kind of golf an exhilarating challenge. But there is also subtly of design and the overwhelming sense of occasion to contend with, and it is my intention to honour all of the elements that make playing Scottish Golf links so rewarding.

— Iain Macfarlane Lowe

THE GRAND MATCH OF 1857.

Scottish Golf Links

The journey Iain Macfarlane Lowe has taken around the linksland of Scotland with his camera is both informative and lyrical—a true labour of love. His photographs capture the heartbeat, the eccentricity and textures of courses which have become unique as many more are constructed or "manufactured" around the world today. You could say that the major courses of great historical interest were laid out on prime Scottish golfing real-estate. The natural contours of the terrain in those early days dictated where to tee off and where to putt out!

Linksland—the link between the sea and the arable ground, where golf, goff, gowf or kolven has been played for centuries. The only patch of rough sandy dune when, in the 15th century, "glub struck featherie and wis retrieved" (club struck ball, was found—and play continued!). Course maintenance was rare and earth moving unheard of.

In Scotland from the east coastline of the Firth of Forth lie many truly great historical links courses such as North Berwick, Gullane, Musselburgh and Muirfield. They still stand proud looking over to Lundin Links, Leven, Elie and Crail in The Kingdom of Fife, on to what has been for centuries the pilgrims trail to St. Andrews. From the 'Home of Golf', on a distant tide line can be seen four long established links including the championship course at Carnoustie on the Tay Estuary. Following this rugged coast up to Montrose and on to the equally imposing sights of Cruden Bay and Royal Aberdeen. From heather, whin and sand, to points north and many more courses, the most significant and acclaimed being Nairn and Dornoch. They are all true links, originating on rough ground that was reclaimed or bequeathed as the game developed and became popular with the gentry. It is a similar story on the west coast of the linksland around Prestwick and Troon. In recent years the links golf trail has become as popular as "the whisky trail" of Scotland.

Early Days

As a form of recreation and leisure, golf was a brisk walk by the seashore with the occasional target or landmark to try to reach with a playclub and wooden or feather ball in the early fifteenth century. Before that it is not fanciful to suggest that shepherds used their crooks to hit stones around the links while tending their sheep or guarding their rabbit warrens! As is human nature, a competitive element emerged as to who could hit the furthest or reach a designated area in the fewest swipes, and so the game evolved. Four centuries later, trains linked up the land in the 1840s and with the new gutta ball being introduced—suddenly the course was accessible and the ball affordable. The links were no longer just the playground for those of inherent wealth—gentlemen of leisure!

The twelve established or recognisable clubs of that era competed against each other in 1857 in the first "Grand Tournament". By 1875, in recognition of young Tom Morris's achievements in golf and his untimely death aged 24, a monument was erected in his memory. The reason for mentioning this epitaph is that it was contributed to by the sixty clubs (and therefore many new courses) in existence by then. In 1890, Willie Park Jr., whose father had won the first Open in 1860, advertised himself as being available for "golf course design and reconstruction". Five years later, and still very much in his prime as a player, Park Jr. declined to compete in the championship at St. Andrews despite having won it twice. His reason was "pressure of work". During this time Tom Morris Sr., then in his seventies, ambled around the country from the most northerly point in Scotland to the most southerly in England and across the sea to Ireland. He set up, or laid out, sixty-nine courses officially credited to him, in what seemed a most casual manner. Morris, usually armed with an armful of seagull feathers, would simply stick them in the ground at an appropriate spot for a tee and let the natural contours around it dictate where the green should lie. One pound a day plus expenses was his fee—the same charge that he and Allan Robertson received for suggesting how a ten hole course at Carnoustie should look in 1848. Not increasing his fee after all those years was Morris's way of giving back to the game that had been his life over such a long and dramatic period in its evolution. "This course will be as good as you want to make it," he would say to the assembled founder members of yet another newly formed club. By the time he retired as keeper of the green, custodian of the links of St. Andrews in 1902, sixteen hundred courses were spread throughout the United Kingdom. At the same time in America the game had taken off and there was mass immigration to The States by accomplished players, club makers and all those who professed to having "laid out a green"!

— David Joy

9

The Scottish Golf Links

ARRANGED BY GEOGRAPHICAL REGION

S T. ANDREWS OLD COURSE AND TOWN. TO THE
RIGHT THE 17TH "ROADHOLE", TO THE FRONT
THE 1ST GREEN PROTECTED BY THE SWILKEN BURN
AND IN THE SHADOWS THE 18TH GREEN.

St. Andrews, or "The Metropolis of Golf" as it was known in the seventeenth and eighteenth centuries, has withstood the test of time despite a constant battle against it! Technology versus tradition—tradition versus technology? Nowhere in the world is there a stretch of land with more of a sense of theatre about it than the Old Course. Imagine members of the Society of St. Andrews Golfers in red jackets with goosenecked clubs tucked under arms, piping through the centre of town from the cobbled end of Market Street. Accompanied by half the population of the city, the gentlemen would assemble on the first tee at 10:00 a.m. for the start of their spring and autumn meetings in the 1760s. Remember great past Open champions such as Bobby Jones holing out for victory in 1927 and being carried shoulder-high off the last green, with putter held aloft, for fear of it being broken by an overexuberant crowd.

In the first Open hosted by St. Andrews, crowds gathered in anticipation of a fifth win in a row by Tom Morris Jr., but it wasn't to be. Arnold Palmer had just failed to win in the Centenary Open in 1960, whipping the galleries into a frenzy when he stormed back into contention from a seven-shot deficit. After a distinguished career he waved, with dignity, an emotional farewell to competitive golf from the Swilken Bridge on the last hole of the Old Course, 35 years later. The "olé" of Seve Ballesteros as he birdied the 18th to a deafening roar is a lasting image, as was the hugely nostalgic parade of past champions down the first and last two holes on the eve of Tiger Wood's millennium victory. Four double-winners of the championship on the Old Course left their mark—Bob Martin, a local caddie and club maker in 1875 and '86, and J. H. Taylor and James Braid at the turn of the century. Jack Nicklaus joined them when he held the claret jug aloft in front of the Royal and Ancient Clubhouse for the second time in 1978.

DUNDEE ■

St. Andrews ●
St. Andrews Bay ●
Kingsbarns ●

Crail ●

Lundin Links ● Elie ●
Leven Links ●

Firth of Forth

1

St. Andrews & The Kingdom of Fife

THE OLD COURSE THE ONLY FLAW IN BOBBY JONES'S RECORD-BREAKING WIN IN THE 1927 OPEN WAS THAT HE DROVE INTO CHEAPES BUNKER FROM THE SECOND TEE THREE ROUNDS OUT OF FOUR. IN THE FIRST ROUND HE HAD TO HOLE A 30 FOOT PUTT FOR BOGEY ON THE SECOND GREEN. HE WENT OUT IN 32 AND CAME BACK IN 36 FOR THE FIRST-EVER SCORE UNDER 70 IN THE CHAMPIONSHIP'S HISTORY. THE BUNKER WAS NAMED AFTER GEORGE CHEAPE, WHOSE FAMILY CLAIMED CERTAIN RIGHTS AND PRIVILEGES IN AND AROUND THE COURSE FOR GENERATIONS. GEORGE'S GRANDFATHER WAS ONE OF THE ORIGINAL FOUNDING MEMBERS OF THE ST. ANDREWS SOCIETY OF GOLFERS (THE R&A) IN 1754.

In the Beginning

The linksland, which was to become the Old, New, Jubilee, and Eden courses, was given to the local folk in the year 1120 by King David II to use as they saw fit. It was bequeathed as an apology, a gesture toward the disruption that would be caused to St. Andreans by the construction of a massive cathedral in the heart of the town that would last over 100 years! Muckross, a Pictish name for "headland of swine" or "land of the wild boar," was the original name of this piece of rough ground some 6,000 years before it became a golfing mecca. In a way, St. Andrews has been a pilgrim's city since the founding of the cathedral, when it became the official ecclesiastical capital of Scotland, a walled city that required a pass to enter. It may sound flippant to say that in recent times (over the 150 years) it has changed its image in becoming the Home of Golf. Apart from the University of St. Andrews maintaining its status as the oldest in the country (founded in 1410), the city itself was decimated by the reformation in the sixteenth century and completely run down by the turn of the eighteenth century. Golf gave it a new lease on life and prosperity as the game and its popularity rose.

The course emerged from a wild, thickly whinned and duned area that protected sheep from winter's piercing, North Sea wind. Hazards like bunkers formed by cattle sheltering, walkways suggested fairways by fishermen taking their long daily walk out to the Eden Estuary to claim mussels for their baited lines, a few flattened areas where rabbits were bred; all contributed to the evolution of the Old Course.

The first map of the course, shaped appropriately like a shepherd's crook, was plotted out in 1754 when the Society of St. Andrews Golfers was formed. The club's name was changed after patronage by King William IV in 1834, to the Royal and Ancient.

They were to have a major influence and, at times, the sole decision on how the Old Course would develop, though the links belonged to the town. Ten years after playing their first spring and autumn meetings, the society decided that the opening four holes were short in length, and merged them into two. Prior to that, the map had shown 11 holes out to the point where one simply turned around and played the same holes back, inward players having the right-of-way. With so few golfers about, this "giving way" was a perfect chance to catch up on worldly affairs or just gossip as they waited their turn on the green!

St. Andrews has become the "Home of Golf" mainly due to the R&A's involvement with the game's progression. To coincide with their 100th anniversary in 1854, the imposing clubhouse behind the first tee was built. By 1897 the R&A had become the guiding light and the governing body of the rules of golf, and from 1920 took over the sole responsibility of running the Open Championship.

On its 250th anniversary year in 2004, H.R.H. the Duke of York, Prince Andrew, became its sixth royal captain. The R&A Foundation, set up in the same year, estimates that it will distribute £50 million by the year 2010 in worldwide funding for the development of golf in surpluses generated from the Open Championship.

THE OLD COURSE LOOKING BACK FROM THE SECOND GREEN GUARDED BY TWO ECCENTRIC HUMPS, A LINE OF WHIN OR GORSE CAN BE SEEN THAT WILL FOLLOW YOU MOST OF THE WAY ROUND THE RIGHT HAND SIDE OF THE COURSE UNTIL IT RUNS OUT OF ROOM JUST SHORT OF THE SIXTEENTH TEE.

FROM THE 5TH TEE, THE GORSE BLOCKS
OUT MOST OF THE HAZARDS SO TAKE AIM
JUST LEFT OF THE SPECTACLE BUNKER IN THE
DISTANCE TO AVOID THE SEVEN SISTERS.

The Fifth Hole

The Seven Sisters await, out of sight from a drive that strays right of centre on the par-5 5th. They are a group of bunkers, shaped in the mid-1880's from heavily sanded waste ground that came into play when more ground was acquired in 1870. Today they are deep, steeply riveted and formidable. The Sisters were probably the first artificial hazards to be put in place on the Old Course—rather than extending or maintaining what nature intended.

The scare caused by the new bounding ball introduced in 1902 forced Hugh Hamilton, who had just taken over from Tom Morris as Keeper of the Green, to scatter small pot bunkers about the course, supposedly to protect it against the longer drives struck with the Haskell ball. The main competitors in the 1905 Open Championship complained bitterly about the new additions, describing them as "spittoons." Despite the extra length achieved with the new ball, the Open was won by nine shots more than were played when, in 1900, St. Andrews had hosted the championship in more agreeable conditions. Thankfully, in 1905 adverse weather had its say in protecting the reputation of the course, as indeed it has done on so many other occasions.

The Spectacles, two alarmingly steep-faced bunkers cut into a ridge guarding the biggest putting green in the world, have to be avoided on the fifth. This is the most famous of the Old Course double greens, sharing with the 13th. It was described as the truest and finest in the country as far back as 1850.

THE OLD COURSE THREE OF THE SEVEN SISTERS BUNKERS.

A DEEP GULLEY PROTECTS THE FRONT OF THE 5TH GREEN, SAID TO BE THE LARGEST IN THE WORLD.

The Old Course is the one destination that all architects feel compelled to visit, and this is not through any feeling of nostalgia. It is, quite simply, the oldest existing example of a golf course laid out on existing terrain, which still provides challenge and excitement for all levels of golfers. When all of the history and emotion is stripped away it stands as a balanced, traditional links course that offers a risk and reward approach to nearly every hole. The first time visitor is often lulled into a false sense of security when confronted by the, at times, 100-yard-wide double fairways and enormous double greens; the double greens always add up to 18 for example: 2 and 16, 3 and 15 etc. This initial view is often altered with the blind and semi-blind tee shots and cavernous bunkers. It is, therefore, wise to play The Old Course a number of times, and then hopefully its architectural merit will become apparent.

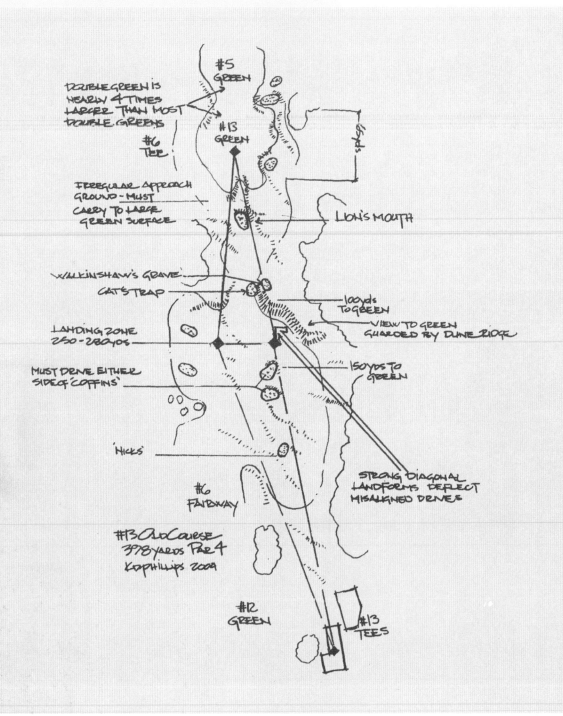

THIS PHOTOGRAPH GIVES A BIRDS EYE VIEW
OF THE LAYOUT AND HAZARDS OF THE 13TH
TO COMPLIMENT THE ARCHITECTURAL DIAGRAM

• GREEN

LION'S MOUTH

CAT'S TRAP

• COFFINS

"As the going gets tough" — History

In all 26 Opens played on the Old since 1873, championship contenders, unknown and established, have stood on the 13th tee thinking, "Just par the last six holes and you'll have a chance." Having picked up shots around the loop (seventh to the twelfth) many scores have been ruined on the homeward trail. Following-in the skyline of the town, the last six holes are fraught with danger. In the first 10 tournaments up to 1900, level-sixes was the average score for the last third of the round! Starting back, the Coffins or Nick's Bunker might grab your ball off the tee on the 13th, or the Lion's Mouth up by the green. All the bunkers on the course have names, some more disturbing than others. On the fourteenth, having avoided the Beardies (or as one Japanese photographer mistakenly named them, "where the bear dies"), Hell Bunker waits for you to try to play around or over it.

The wind conditions are a major factor in how the course plays on any links course, but nowhere more so than at St. Andrews. Because of the shape of the course, more often than not a sea breeze will blow you right to left all the way out from the second hole and vice versa all the way in from the 12th. The winds can be strong and unpredictable, turning right around during the course of a round. For example, Tony Lema owed part of his championship win to playing the first round in 1964 before a gale blew up, in what Jack Nicklaus described as the worst conditions he ever had to play in, setting off in the draw three hours after the eventual winner.

St. Andrews Old #13 — Architecture

Locals say that the true challenge of The Old Course starts on the 13th tee. The tee shot offers the immediate hazard of Nick's Bunker and The Coffins, positioned between the 13th and 6th fairway and this is the risk and reward option. Take on and clear the bunkers and an easy approach shot to this largest of greens is your reward. Any tee shot right of the bunkers, avoiding the line of gorse all down the right side of the fairway, must not end up too close to the six foot high plateau that protudes into the fairway and can block the view of the approach shot. This is the least hazardous route from the tee but leaves a longer approach shot bringing green-side bunkers more into play.

Opposite, top: The tee shot on the 13th offers a simple choice. The easier shot of staying to the right of Nicks' Bunker and The Coffins (the 13th fairway) provides a more challenging and longer approach to the green. Going left, over the bunkers, onto the 6th fairway holds more risks but gives a far easier and shorter second shot. Both choices offer classic risks and rewards.

Right: Approaching the "Cats Trap", this little bunker just on the back of a ridge is not even seen by 99% of golfers but for those unlucky few it may take imagination and more than a little luck to escape on the first attempt. This was not a posed shot.

Far right: Approaching the 13th green (red flag) from the 6th fairway offers a far easier opportunity to the pin.

This aerial view in the low light of autumn captures part of the aura of the most famous linksland in the world. The ancient city of St. Andrews and rolling waves from the North Sea, caused by the aftermath of a storm, add an atmospheric backdrop. In the foreground, The Old Course fourteenth hole and fifth running parallel to it, are flanked to the left and right by the third of the New course and second of the Eden, with part of the Jubilee nearest the shoreline.

14TH TEE TO GREEN. THE DAWN LIGHT DRAMATISES THE SPRING COLOURS AROUND THE 14TH TEE SWEEPING DOWN THE FAIRWAY TO THE TOWN BEYOND.

Fourteenth

The Elysian Fields, so named as the only respite on the course on the way out was a welcome flat piece of ground to the seventeenth or eighteenth-century golfer, for it was devoid of towering whin and coarse grass invading it. Played in "the original way," you drove over Hell to it on route for the fifth green. The significance of its name is lost because the course through time has become "more sociable" or less hostile. The end of a good drive off the 14th is now the same spot before a daunting carry over the renowned Hell Bunker. This yawning chasm has varied in its depth but not its shape throughout the ages. Funding was sought in the 1880s to stop the erosion of many of the bunkers by riveting or banking them. It was yet another time of change for the course, though most of it superficial, as the first lawnmower was introduced! One old worthy member of the R&A complained to the greens committee that, "with the width of the fairway today one can simply skirt 'round the hazards, to which sir, I protest vehemently, as this most definitely is not how the game should be played."

THE PAR 5 14TH VIEW OF HELL BUNKER 2002 — 22 PACES FROM LEFT TO RIGHT, 20 PACES FRONT TO BACK AND WITH THE FRONT WALL OVER 6 FEET HIGH! — AND — COMPARISON VIEW OF HELL BUNKER 1890 (ABOVE).

The 17th has been the most talked-about hole in golf since the first pint of blackstrap (a stout) was poured in the Auld Union Parlour behind the last green in 1826! A book has been recently published which is solely devoted to stories of triumph and (mostly) disaster on it. The old railway yards' black sheds, used to store hickory and coal on Station Park from 1852, were replaced by a luxury British Rail hotel in 1967—two years later, they closed down the line into the town! The Old Course Hotel has since been added too, making it look an even more daunting drive than it was before, with the worry of going out-of-bounds in it. The hole was played as a par-5 up until the 1964 Open, which then enhanced the trauma it would inflict in going for the green as a par-4. Up to that point in time it was wise to just lay up short right of the infamous Road Hole bunker and the Devil's Swale or avoid the bumpy road directly behind this unreceptive narrow green. John Ball, the first Englishman to win the Open, much to the delight of the local spectators, took 13 here when in contention defending the championship he had won at Prestwick in 1890. Only 10 feet from the flag, he jumped like a pinball from rut to rut on the old road until he finally made the green, 30 yards from the hole, eight shots later.

425 yards blind, dog-leg right, narrow long green at right angles to the fairway, one deep pot bunker to the front (with gathering contours), a road directly behind the green and out-of bounds wall just beyond. This is the 17th on St. Andrews Old Course, arguably the most famous hole in golf and one that challenges the abilities of all golfers.

The totally blind tee shot over the old railway sheds is intimidating, everything right being out of bounds and anything too straight or left will run through the fairway into long grass. Even from the fairway the approach shot, with a medium to long iron, seems akin to threading a needle.

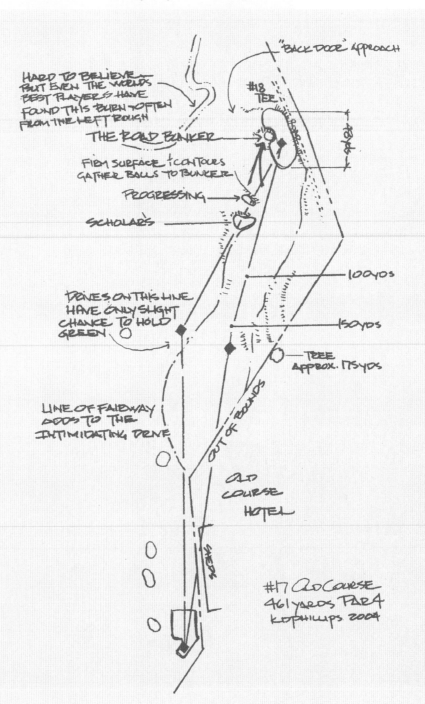

THE 17TH TEE REQUIRES A BLIND SHOT OVER THE
FACING SHEDS. TOO FAR RIGHT AND THE HOTEL IS A CASU-
ALTY AND YOUR BALL IS, INVARIABLY, LOST. TOO FAR LEFT
LEAVES AN UNREACHABLE DISTANCE FROM THE GREEN.

APPROACH TO THE 17TH ROAD HOLE WITH SCHOLARS
BUNKER TO THE LEFT. THE APPROACH TO THE GREEN IS
HEAVILY CONTOURED, WITH ANYTHING SLIGHTLY LEFT GEN-
TLY GUIDED INTO THE FAMOUS AND GENERALLY PAINFUL
"ROADHOLE BUNKER"

THE ROADHOLE BUNKER CAUSES EXTREMES OF EMO-
TION. ABSOLUTE DISMAY AS YOUR BALL DISAPPEARS
INTO ITS DEPTHS OR MAYBE RELIEF IF IT IS THAT OF YOUR
MATCH-PLAY OPPONENT; FRUSTRATION AS YOUR BALL FALLS
BACK TO YOUR FEET AFTER THAT FIRST, AND MAYBE SUBSE-
QUENT, ATTEMPT TO ESCAPE FAILS. FOR ALL OTHERS IT IS
A PASSING CURIOSITY AND MAYBE A PHOTO OPPORTUNITY.

Scottish Golf Links

There is nothing more relaxing, after a brisk walk out the West Sands and back at low tide, than to look out "from whence you came," comfortable with whisky in hand, in the lounge of the St. Andrews Golf Club. As the last green and Royal and Ancient clubhouse are bathed in late summer light, images of great drama watched by huge crowds, echo around this familiar scene.

THE IMPOSING 12TH CENTURY CATHEDRAL, EVEN IN THIS STATE OF RUIN, DOMINATES THE SKYLINE TO THE SOUTH OF THE TOWN AND STAND AS A STARK REMINDER TO ST. ANDREWS EARLY DAYS.

The Town of St. Andrews

While wandering around the ruins of what was the largest cathedral in Scotland until plundered during the sixteenth century Reformation, you may stumble upon seven relatively recent graves of past Open Champions. Allan Robertson, known as the world's first golf professional, is buried here, as is the first captain of the R&A. Robertson was a ball maker in a house by the corner of the eighteenth green, as was his father and his grandfather before him up until "yon new fangled gutta baw" took over their trade in 1849. He was never beaten in foursomes, partnered by Tom Morris, who started his long and illustrious career as a feather ball maker with Allan. From 1842 up until Robertson's untimely death at age 42 in 1859, they held off the challenge of the Park brothers from Musselburgh and the Dunn's from North Berwick in many much-publicised matches. In the shadow of the square tower lie father and son, young and old Tom Morris—both four-time winners of the Open. Young Tom died on Christmas Day in 1875, aged twenty-four while his father lived on another 32 years and became "The Grand Old Man of Golf."

Still in the cathedral grounds is the tomb of Sir Hugh Lyon Playfair, chief magistrate and provost of St. Andrews, who single-handedly took this run-down town by the scruff of the neck and whipped it back into shape! In 1843 he printed and distributed 50 rules "that must be obeyed." For example, "No one will be allowed more than one ton of dung around their premise during the months of May to September, inclusive." Sir Hugh was formidable. He was responsible for all major changes in the heart of the city, from organising the building of four new streets with a whiff of opulent Georgian Edinburgh about them to attract people of wealth and status back into the town, to the erection of a splendid town hall. He solved the sewage problem and widened the streets. He formed the St. Andrews Railway Company in 1851 and had the locals build their own track to join up with the main line; three miles away—he even bought the train to go with it!

From the cathedral ruins, images are conjured up of King James V marrying Mary of Guise there   or, over 200 years before that, Robert the Bruce riding down the central isle to consecrate the building and give thanks to God for his victory at Bannockburn in 1318. Everywhere you turn around the old city centre, layers of antiquity reveal themselves. The university, the first seat of learning in Scotland—the castle, that schooled the young Kings James II and IV in the fifteenth century—the great wall and gates, at which you needed a pass to enter, and were then recognised as the ecclesiastical capital of Scotland.

Today, St. Andrews is lively and prosperous. As the tourist season finishes in the end of October, back come 6,000 students from their summer break to keep the old grey city lively through its long winter months. In the summer, the pubs in or around Golf Place (just a wedge from the eighteenth green) are full of visiting golfers who might well be drinking a toast to their first round on the Old Course or breaking 90 or even 80 on it! Others that have gotten lucky in the ballot and secured a time on the Old for the next day may feel the need to do likewise!

The one big problem in the peak months of summer is the availability of tee times on the Old, or the lack of them, in a ballot system where you take your chance and hope you make the draw. If unlucky, there is still an abundance of premier links courses to play in and around this area, as you will see as this section of the book unfolds.

COMPARISON AERIAL VIEWS OF THE TOWN OF ST. ANDREWS. ONE LOOKING THROUGH THE CATHEDRAL RUINS OUT TOWARDS THE LINKS AND THE OTHER THROUGH THE OLD WEST PORT AND OUT TOWARDS THE CATHEDRAL AND THE HARBOUR.

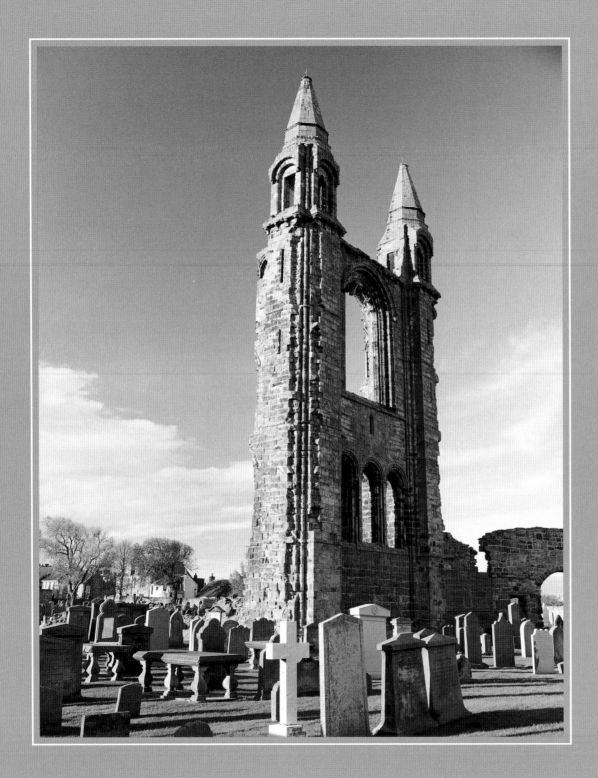

YOUNG TOM'S GRAVE, IN THE CATHEDRAL GROUNDS, WAS CONTRIBUTED TO BY SIXTY CLUBS AFTER HIS UNTIMELY DEATH IN 1875.

BENEATH THE SOD POOR TOMMY'S LAID
BUNKERED NOW FOR GOOD AND ALL;
A BETTER GOLFER NEVER HIT
A FURTHER OR A SURER BALL
AMONG THE MONARCHS O' THE GREEN
FOR LONG HE HELD IMPERIAL SWAY;
AND NONE, THE START AND END BETWEEN
COULD MATCH WITH TOMMY ON HIS DAY.

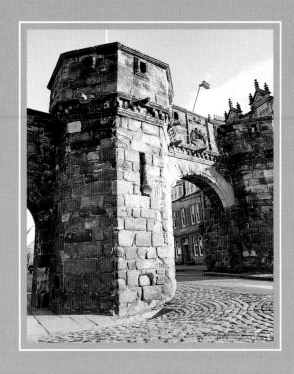

THE WEST PORT, THE CASTLE RUINS, CATHEDRAL AND ST. SALVATORS, ARE JUST SOME OF THE ANCIENT BUILDINGS THAT STOOD PROUD AND IMPOSING PRIOR TO THE MID 16TH CENTURY REFORMATION. WHAT REMAINS IS STONEWORK PITTED BY CENTURIES OF EROSION AND THE SCARS OF MAN'S STRUGGLE THROUGH ST. ANDREWS LONG AND CHEQUERED HISTORY. THE ONLY WAY TO CAPTURE THE TEXTURES AND A SENSE OF THE HISTORIC PAST IS IN BLACK AND WHITE.

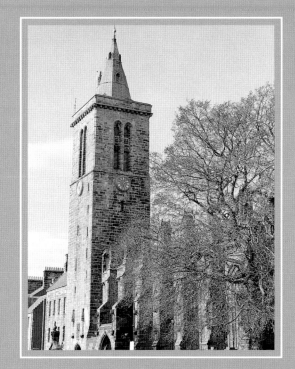

THE NEW COURSE THE 4TH, BLIND FROM THE TEE, IS A PAR FOUR SLIGHT DOGLEG LEFT WITH THE GREEN PROTECTED, TO THE FRONT, BY THREE POT BUNKERS. TO THE LEFT OF PICTURE IS THE PAR THREE 5TH TEE TO GREEN.

9TH TEE TO GREEN, PAR THREE. NO BUNKERS, OUT OF BOUNDS TO THE LEFT AND THE GREEN IN A NATURAL BOWL.

ST. ANDREWS LINKS

When the old town council was disbanded in 1973 a links trust was set up to protect the rights of local people and take on the responsibility of the upkeep of the courses.

Since then, two new courses, a modern practice facility, and two clubhouses for the visiting golfer have been added to keep up with the ever-rising demand for play. Over 200,000 rounds are played each year, helping to generate an income of over £10 million pounds. As a charitable organisation, the Links Trust does not pay taxes because all profits are used to maintain and protect the future of the whole facility.

THE JUBILEE COURSE OPENED IN 1897 INTENDED FOR LADIES AND JUNIORS IT HAD, AT THAT TIME, JUST 12 HOLES. IT IS A COURSE THAT HAS EXPERIENCED ALMOST CONTINUAL CHANGE AND, ALMOST 100 YEARS AFTER ITS INCEPTION, IT WAS AGAIN CHANGED TO THE COURSE WE KNOW TODAY. RECOGNISED IN TOWN AS THE TOUGHEST OF THE FIVE HOME COURSES, IT NOW MEASURES UP TO 6,800 YARDS AND IS ROUTED CLOSEST TO THE LONG WEST SANDS BEACH.

The New Course

The New Course, running parallel to the right of the Old, was officially opened the day after St. Andrews hosted the 1895 Open. The winner, J.H.Taylor, and the top 20 finishers played to set the course record. Eighty-five was the best score by the 1891 Open Champion, local man Hugh Kirkaldy. Comments in the press the next week by the players were generally that they considered it more difficult to score on than the Old and that "the hazards were quite frightening." Tom Morris laid out the course with a budget of £100 per hole, mostly financed by the R&A. The course today still has its greens in their original positions; apart from lengthening it, no major changes have been made.

The New was used in qualifying for the Open from 1921 to 1970. Up until the Centenary Open, two qualifying rounds were played on Tuesday and four rounds (if you made the cut) by Thursday, so that the professionals could be back at their home club in time to organise the members' times for Saturday!

The Jubilee Course

Two years after the New opened it was the Queen's Diamond Jubilee. Tom Morris was again asked to lay out another course to alleviate the pressure of play during the summer months. This time his remit was to make it a 12-hole course suitable for the novice or lady golfer, with a budget of £12 per hole. It was soon converted to 18 holes and through the years eminent course designers H.S. Colt and Donald Steel have had a hand in reshaping what is now considered by locals as the most difficult of all the courses to score on from medal tees.

THE EDEN COURSE **ABOVE**: APPROACH TO THE 7TH GREEN. **BELOW**: 5TH TEE TO GREEN

The Eden Course

In 1914 The Eden Course opened—again to absorb the ever-increasing demand for more golf. H. S. Colt was sought after, and eventually agreed to lay out the course. He was probably the most underrated golf architect of his day. Colt is often talked about by his fellow designers today as one of the true geniuses of golf course architecture. While the Eden was under construction, Colt was in partnership with Alister MacKenzie and also working on two courses in the States (one of them with Donald Ross), one in Canada and another in England that year!

By 1920 the Eden had hosted its own tournament, which became a major match play competition on the Scottish circuit. The course was revamped in 1989 but retains some of its old charm and Harry Colt magic. It still meanders in part around the Eden Estuary with its old whins and dunes intact.

The Strathtyrum and Balgrove Courses

Part of the old Strathtyrum estate originally owned by Archbishop Sharpe in the seventeenth century now accommodates the short 18-hole course, which was constructed in 1993 to cope with the popularity of the game and to provide an easier test of golf than its four big brothers. The nine-hole Balgove course was put in place the same year as an introduction to golf for the young or late starter.

The Seasons

It is a rare event if a heavy snowfall prevents play here, but a hard white early morning frost frequently does in the deep midwinter. From biting winds and driving rain to the heralding of spring, when whins in bright yellow bloom, lining nearly every fairway; from patches of green grass and unpredictable bounce during long summer days to low, light purple heather and the golden whispy rough of autumn. Of course, the Old and every other links in Scotland can throw all the seasons, weatherwise, at you in one round!

THE HAAR (MIST OR FOG) ROLLS IN AND ADDS A FIFTH SEASON WHEN FLAGS, GREENS AND FAIRWAYS MERGE WITH WHIN AND HEATHER.

The Links of the Kingdom of Fife

The Kingdom (as in "the king's domain" of the fourteenth century), with St. Andrews as the jewel in its crown, has a royal family of links courses to back up its name. Now there are 48 courses of varying shapes and sizes spread throughout this small county. On a 14 mile trip alone, along the east coastline of Fife with a constant, but ever-changing smell and sound of the seashore, stand 10 of them: from Leven and Lundin Links where the local right to play over the Dubbieside links for centuries was made official with the formation of their clubs in 1846 and 1847—to the Golf House, Elie, where originally a charter confirmed old privileges such as "the right of golf" there in 1589; past Anstruther with a nine-hole course over 100 years old to Crail—the seventh oldest golf club in Scotland—to Kingsbarns and a stunning new links course on an old site. From St. Andrews Bay another two new courses are perched up on its cliff line with 60 mile views across the Tay Estuary and Sidlaw Hills to the Grampian Mountains.

LEVEN LINKS

In the spring meeting of 1848 the first new gutta ball caused a stir when seen in competition on what was then called the Dubbieside Links. Verse of a song at that time: "These velvet links of golfers rife, Are they in Paradise or Fife? Am I alive or have I died, Or am I not at Dubbieside?" The course played host to the first Open Amateur Stroke Play Competition in 1870. Two years before, young and old Tom Morris played a 36-hole match to commemorate the course's conversion from nine holes to 18. Young Tom, having just won his first Open at Prestwick at age 17, scored 170 on the new Leven course to beat his father by 17 shots. Three clubs shared the links at that time - the Innerleven Golfing Society being the oldest when, in 1820, they played their first spring medal of three five-hole rounds in uniformed jackets of King Charles tartan. Both Leven and Lundin Links have been used as qualifying courses for the Open at St. Andrews since 1978.

A visiting American sportsman, Mr. Whitney, described his reaction to the Leven course in 1894—"The surface of the ground looks like one vast, irregular succession of congealed sandwaves!"

ONE HUNDRED AND TWENTY YEARS AGO "THE BUS" OR COACH (ABOVE) WAS STILL LEAVING ST. ANDREWS ONCE A DAY FOR CRAIL VIA KINGSBARNS. EIGHT PASSENGERS ON TOP, EXPOSED TO THE ELEMENTS, AND SIX TRAVELLERS INSIDE THE COACH, PULLED BY THREE HORSES. UNTIL THE COAST RAILWAY LINKED UP EAST FIFE IN 1887, IT WAS HARDLY SURPRISING THAT LOCAL GOLFERS DIDN'T VENTURE MUCH FURTHER FROM THEIR HOME COURSE.

LEVEN LINKS OLD RAILWAY SLEEPERS SUP-
PORT THE BANK FROM COLLAPSE AND ADD TO THE
CHALLENGE OF REACHING THE GREEN SAFELY.
BELOW: LOOKING BACK THROUGH THE 2ND GREEN.

LUNDIN LINKS THE 2ND, SEPARATED FROM THE SEA BY PROTECTIVE DUNES, IS A WELL BUNKERED AND UNDULATING PAR 4. **RIGHT**: APPROACH TO THE 10TH GREEN PROTECTED BY THIS ISLAND BUNKER. **BELOW**: LETTER FROM JAMES BRAID (INSET) TO LUNDIN LINKS GOLF CLUB, 30TH APRIL 1908. 7TH LINE ON READS "ON THE OTHER COURSE [LUNDINS PROPOSED

NEW EXTENSION] THE GROUND IS TOO UNDULATING TO MARK THEM (THE BUNKERS) ON THE PLAN AS THE CHIEF POINT IN MAKING BUNKERS IS TO GET THEM SO THAT THEY DRAW TOWARDS THEM AS MUCH AS POSSIBLE. MAKE THEM FAIRLY LARGE AS SOME OF THOSE ON THE PRESENT COURSE ARE FAR TOO SMALL."

& Cruickshank. Esq   30th April 1908

Memorandum from **JAMES BRAID,**

OPEN CHAMPION, 1901.
       "   "   1905.
       "   "   1906.

WALTON HEATH GOLF CLUB,
WALTON-ON-THE-HILL, Surrey.

GOLF CLUB and **BALL MAKER.**

STATION:—
Tadworth, S.E.Ry.

Telegrams:—"BRAID, GOLF, WALTON-ON-THE-HILL."

PARCELS:—Tadworth Station, S.E.Ry.

Speciality: DRIVERS and BRASSIES.

Dear Sir / Herewith I enclose you the plans of the two courses which you sent me. I have marked the bunkers on the Ladies course, which you will perhaps kindly enter on plan, as you will do it better than I will. I don't advise the making of them all until the course has been played on make those round the greens and some at the long holes on the other course. the ground is too undulating to mark them on the plan, as the chief point in making bunkers is so that they draw towards them as much ... fairly large as some of these on

LUNDIN LINKS

The shared links of the Leven and Lundin clubs (1,000 and 400 members) became congested by 1907. The following year, having acquired more prime links, James Braid, fresh from his fourth out of five wins in the Open, arrived to lay out a new course. He had already visited the proposed site, for he was born and raised just four miles down the road and knew the area well, having played much of his golf there as a boy. Here is an extract from a letter from him to the Lundin club that year.

> "The first five holes are typical links holes skirting the waters edge. The next nine over the now defunct railway line are a mixture of parkland and links turf, while the last four holes go back towards the sea and have a more traditional look about them."

LUNDIN LINKS VIEW FROM THE ELEVATED 14TH TEE ONTO THE PANORAMA OF LUNDIN LINKS. IN THE FOREGROUND THE 10TH GREEN WITH THE 4TH AND 5TH HOLES BEYOND; TO THE EXTREME RIGHT "MILE DYKE" WALL AND LEVEN'S 4TH GREEN ON THE OTHER SIDE.

APASSING STORM BREAKS AND A SHAFT OF SUN-LIGHT CASTS A SHADOW ACROSS THE HILL. IT'S AN UNSETTLING BLIND TEE SHOT FOR THE FIRST DRIVE ON THE COURSE. THE PERISCOPE EMERGING FROM THE STARTER'S HUT IS AN UNUSUAL FEATURE.

ELIE

In the starter's box by the first tee, a submariner's periscope was installed in 1966 to spot when the fairway was clear for the next match to play. The blind opening drive had caused problems. In the past a mirror was placed strategically up on the clubhouse chimney, or before that in the 1920s a boy stood on top of the hill waving a flag, indicating when it was safe to play! The Golf House Club formed in 1875 boasts an array of distinguished captains. Right Honourables, Sirs, Earls, Majors, a Brigadier, a General, and a Colonel have all held office. J. E. Laidlay was a captain of note in 1896, having won the British Amateur Championship twice at St. Andrews and been runner-up at Prestwick. Five-time winner of the Open, James Braid, was a scratch golfer by the age of 16 on this course shared by his homeclub Earlsferry Thistle in 1886.

ELIE CLOUDS MIRRORED ON THE FORTH ESTUARY PROVIDE
A DRAMATIC BACKDROP TO THE 6TH GREEN.

ELIE. LOOKING DOWN ON THE 13TH GREEN AND AROUND THE SWEEP OF THE BAY TO THE 12TH GREEN. BEYOND ARE THE 15TH, 9TH AND 6TH GREENS WITH 11TH, A PAR 3, OUT ON THE HEADLAND. TO THE FAR LEFT ARE THE 5TH AND 7TH GREENS.

Crail Golfing Society was founded in 1786, making it one of the 10 oldest clubs in the world. Initially they played on a narrow strip of shore land where they managed to lay out eight holes. In early days Leith had five holes, St. Andrews and Musselburgh nine, Prestwick 12, Carnoustie 10 and Montrose from 13 to 22! It was only in the 1870s that 18 holes became standard for a round. Many courses had nine holes that were played twice, and Crail followed suit when, in 1895, Tom Morris was invited to lay out a new nine-hole course on the Balcomie Links. It ran alongside the old Sauchope Links where golf had been played for over three centuries.

Crail was quick to convert to 18 holes after just one bazaar raised more than the sum of £465 needed for their reconstruction. "Grand or Great Bazaars," with their big marquees, stalls, and fiddle bands seemed to be the most civilised and successful way of fund-raising during the Victorian era. The Links have retained their original character, and became so popular for its ambience and vista that another course, the Craighead Links, was opened in 1998 on slightly higher ground, giving a panoramic view from Dunbar to Montrose.

It would seem that golf was played mostly in the winter and spring months up until the 1850s despite its inhospitable climate at times. Farming had a big influence in when the main Autumn Meeting should be. For example, in Crail Golfing Society's minute book, it was announced in 1824 that, due to an early harvest, the meeting would be brought forward.

THE NAME TOM MORRIS WILL CROP UP MANY TIMES ON THIS "PHOTOGRAPHER'S JOURNEY" AROUND SCOTLAND, FOR IN THE 1890S HE WAS INUNDATED WITH REQUESTS FROM NEW OR ESTABLISHED CLUBS TO LOOK AT THEIR COURSES OR PROPOSED SITE FOR ONE.

THE ELEVATED 14TH TEE OFFERS A CLEAR VIEW OF THIS PAR 3 HOLE AS WELL AS A PANORAMA OF THE BALCOMIE COURSE AT CRAIL.

CRAIL **ABOVE:** THE BALCOMBIE COURSE 13TH
IS A MOST CHALLENGING 200 YARD PAR 3.
BELOW: THE COURSE MEANDERS AROUND THE
COASTLINE AS FAR AS THE 5TH GREEN BEFORE
TURNING FOR THE 190 YARD 6TH.

CRAIL **ABOVE:** THE CRAIGHEAD COURSE, OPENED IN 1999, IS PERCHED ON THE CLIFF TOP OVERLOOKING THE FIRTH OF FORTH. IT IS A CONSIDERABLY TOUGHER CHALLENGE THAN THE BALCOMBIE COURSE AND, PERHAPS BEING NEW, DOES NOT HAVE THAT QUIRKY CHARM. **BELOW:** 18TH APPROACH PAR 4.

KINGSBARNS

In 1998, while excavating and converting the original site of the late eighteenth century nine-hole course, a headless bronze-age skeleton was unearthed on what is now the sixteenth ladies tee! Disappointingly, there was no evidence of it being the first green keeper of that era—no sign of goosenecked hickory clubs alongside it. More was revealed as construction took place.

The new Kingsbarns course, "embracing the sea," has received local (the true test) and international praise, dramatically shooting up the world ranking of the top 100 courses. Kyle Phillips, who provides the architectural commentary to this book, was the designer. He and his fellow American developers, Mark Parsinen and Art Dunkley, deserve all the credit for their vision and enhancement of the reputation of the links courses in Scotland. Their message at the launch during the millennium was, "May the heart, soul, and intellect of Kingsbarns be absorbing and provide pleasure to all golfers." It certainly does that.

KINGSBARNS **Opposite**: Aerial view with the clubhouse and 1st tee in the foreground. Just beyond are the 9th green and the 18th green (which is characterised by an abrupt falloff into a burn nestled at its front). On the left is the 16th green and fairway with the 7th and 8th holes to the right of the 16th fairway. On the extreme right is the 10th fairway and green. **Below**: A comparison of the second tee to green before and after. **Above**: This three thousand year old headless skeleton was found very near the 16th fairway.

K INGSBARNS IS THE VISUAL STORY OF THE EXPANDED RE-
BIRTH OF A GOLF COURSE ON A DRAMATIC STRETCH OF
SCOTTISH COASTLINE CLOSE TO ST. ANDREWS. PHOTOGRAPHING
THE CONSTRUCTION OF A NEW LINKS COURSE OFFERED ME A
UNIQUE INSIGHT INTO THE ISSUES THAT AROSE THROUGHOUT
THE EARTH-MOVING AND ARTISTIC CREATION OF THIS PREMIER
COURSE. IT IS DIFFICULT TO TRULY CONVEY ALL OF THIS IN JUST
A FEW PAGES BUT I HOPE THE SELECTED SHOTS MAY GIVE SOME
INSIGHT INTO THE BEFORE AND AFTER. THIS AERIAL VIEW CAP-
TURES THE FULL DRAMA OF LINKS GOLF. WAVES CRASHING ONTO
THE BEACH BESIDE THE 3RD GREEN AND FAIRWAY OF THIS PAR 5.

KINGSBARNS THREE VIEWS SHOWING THE
TRANSFORMATION OF LAND AROUND THE PRESENT
6TH GREEN. **TOP**: IN 1995 A DERELICT OLD BARN AND
WALL MARK THE LOCATION OF THE OLD KINGSBARNS
9 HOLE GOLF COURSE. **BOTTOM**: IMAGINATIVE ROUTING
COMBINE WITH CAREFUL CONSTRUCTION AND SHAPING
AND THE COURSE STARTS TO EMERGE. **OPPOSITE**:
THE 6TH GREEN OFFERS GOLFERS A MOST MEMORABLE
LINKS CHALLENGE AND, WITH A BURN HIDDEN AT THE
BACK, A STING IN THE TAIL.

KINGSBARNS LOOKING BACK THROUGH THE 7TH GREEN TO THE 16TH, 6TH AND 17TH HOLES. **RIGHT**: 13TH TEE TO GREEN PAR 3. FROM THIS ELEVATED TEE, THE GREEN AND ALL OF ITS ISSUES, JUST 148 YARDS AWAY, ARE CLEARLY VISIBLE. **RIGHT, BELOW**: 15TH TEE TO GREEN PAR 3. 212 YARDS FROM THE CHAMPIONSHIP TEES, TREES TO THE LEFT, SEA TO THE RIGHT, SWIRLING WINDS, AND FACING WHAT APPEARS TO BE A SHALLOW GREEN, A DAUNTING SHOT.

With visual contact to the sea from every hole, this new fully constructed links has been universally accepted as an authentic links course by the connoisseurs of golf. Everything about Kingsbarns is uniquely its own, but 'inspiration' has been provided by the some of the great links courses from around the world. Even though each person who contributed is justifiably proud of the final product, I will always see Kingsbarns as a man-made creation lead by divine Providence. A testament to this story is the discovery of the centuries old burn and bridge excavated some nine feet underground beside the 18th green, (inspired by #16 at Turnberry) that were almost to the meter where I had designed a new bridge and burn to be constructed.

Kingsbarns #12

Likened by many to the 18th at Pebble Beach, strategically the 12th at Kingsbarns is, in fact, completely different. The preferred line off the tee is away from the sea and down the right hand side of the fairway, where a strong contour can provide extra length to the shorter, but properly placed drive, feeding the ball back towards the centre of the fairway and neutralizing the advantage of the long player. When attempting to reach the green in two, one must play on a narrow line, flirting with the sea on the left, but always wary of the ancient sea cliff that pinches in on the right of the green. Those who choose to lay back on their second shots should take a line towards the small bunker in the old sea cliff face. If taking a line to right of this bunker, care must be taken not to play too close to the cliff, as from this position a difficult blind 3rd shot awaits. Regardless of which option is executed, club selection will vary greatly on the approach to this 60 yard deep green, depending on the pin placement.

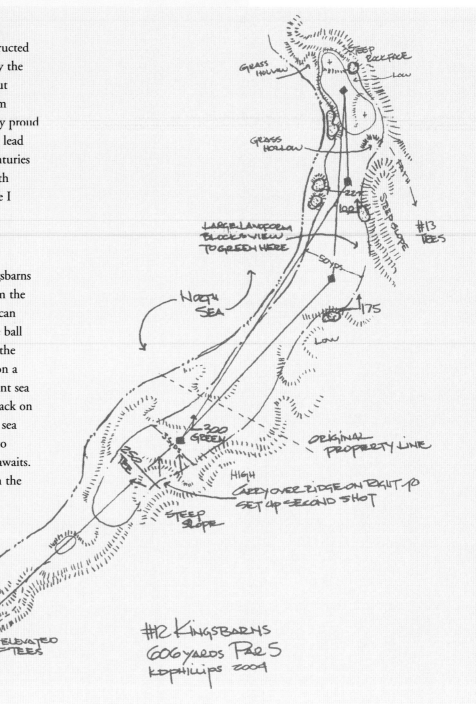

Aerial view of 12th green back up to the tee.

OPPOSITE: THE PAR 5 TWELFTH TEE TO GREEN. BELOW, LEFT:
APPROACH TO THE 12TH. A SOLID TEE SHOT LEAVES A TEMPT-
ING CHOICE. AIM SAFE FOR THE BUNKER ON THE RIGHT OR THE
TIGER LINE ALONG THE COAST. BELOW, RIGHT: ANYTHING TOO
BOLD AND THE BUNKERS ON THE LEFT COME INTO PLAY.

It was decided, early in construction, that the final hole at Kingsbarns would benefit from having a stream protecting the front edge of the green. To this end a search began, near to the present 10th tee, for the source of the outflow further down the course. Just below the surface solid stone slabs were found and, under these, a beautifully constructed dry stone walled river. This feature was excavated as it made its rather erratic way towards the 18th green. With a final twist, the burn, now nine feet under the natural site level, turned directly along the front of the green. To the amazement of all, a bridge was also uncovered and, after some minor repair, it is now once again in use. The green was slightly lowered, but still towers above the water hazard, and the fairway was lowered to gently slope down to the burn. Research discovered that the river was constructed during the first decade of the 1800's, as part of a programme of draining land, it was routed to tie in with a bridge constructed at a much earlier time.

KINGSBARNS TOP: THE STONE-LINED AND COVERED BURN AND BRIDGE ARE UNCOVERED NINE FEET UNDERGROUND. CENTER: SITE MANAGER BARD REYNOLDS (RIGHT) AND CONSTRUCTION MANAGER (NOW HEAD GREENKEEPER) STUART MCCOLM (LEFT) STAND AMONGST THE DEBRIS OF THE DISCOVERY, DISCUSS THE DISCOVERY AND RESHAPING ISSUES. LOWER: THE APPROACH TO THE 18TH GREEN TODAY.

ST. ANDREWS BAY — DEVLIN AERIAL VIEW OF THE DEVLIN COURSE PERCHED ON THE CLIFF TOP. IN THE FOREGROUND THE 11TH GREEN AND THE CLUBHOUSE, IN THE MIDDLE, MARKS THE END THE OF DEVLIN AND START OF THE TORRANCE COURSES. **BELOW**: THE ELEVATED 11TH TEE OFFERS A CLEAR VIEW DOWN TO THE GREEN AND ACROSS THE BAY TO THE OPPOSITE COAST AND CARNOUSTIE GOLF LINKS.

ST. ANDREWS BAY

The Devlin and Torrance courses are a recent asset to this links playground, constructed just two miles south of St. Andrews up on the cliffline by the old coastal path. This walkway from the town has "a right-of-way" through all the courses mentioned and is a leisurely, if not strenuous way to view and get a true sense of linksland and all its diversity—as long as you've arranged to be picked up at the other end!

The Torrance

The Torrance is named after its designer, Sam Torrance, a great golfing ambassador for the Scots and past captain of a winning Ryder Cup team. Its inspiration came from a sketch by the late Gene Sarazen, winner of the British and American Open in 1932. On his last visit to St. Andrews in 1999 he looked at the site with his friend the eventual owner and developer of both the courses and a large hotel and conference centre, Doctor Don Pannoz. This rolling waste and farmland with its spectacular view took shape and has been well used by townsfolk and visitors. The seventeenth signature hole named "Sam's Brawest," utilizes the coastal walk dyke (wall) with a view through a curving cliff line to the skyline and spires of the old grey city.

The Devlin

The Devlin was designed and constructed by Australian Bruce Devlin, who took full advantage of its contours and clifftop hazards in his layout. Devlin is a prolific course designer. In the States he has laid out over 70 courses and reconstructed another 10, but he is no stranger to Scotland. He was fifth in the Open on the Old Course in 1964 and fourth at Muirfield two years later.

ST. ANDREWS BAY — TORRANCE
AERIAL VIEW OF THE TORRANCE COURSE,
HOTEL AND CLUBHOUSE.

And so you find yourself back in St. Andrews, some drawn to it time and time again. The course's and the town's ambience are as unpredictable as its weather! Bobby Jones said in a moving acceptance speech when receiving the Freedom of the City in 1958: "The more I studied the Old Course, the more I loved it…the more I loved it, the more I studied it." He talked from the heart that night, among friends, journalists, and a large turnout of locals at the official presentation in the university's Younger Hall. He finished by saying: "If I could take from my life everything but my experiences at St. Andrews I would still have had a rich and full life."

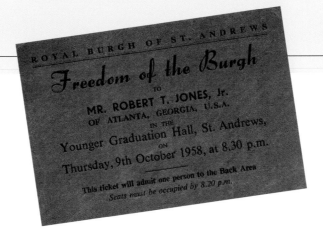

ST. ANDREWS BAY — TORRANCE THE VIEW FROM THE CLUBHOUSE BALCONY OF THE 17TH FAIRWAY AND GREEN. ACROSS THE BAY THE SPIRES AND STEEPLES OF ST. ANDREWS ARE SILHOUETTED AGAINST THE EVENING LIGHT.

Carnoustie was slow in terms of cashing in on the golfing tourist during the Victorian era, and late in hosting the Open Championship for the first time. It was certainly not slow or late in being recognised as a prime strip of Linksland as early as 1502 when Sir Robert Maule, the Earl of Panmure, was spotted "exercising at the gouffe." For over 40 years he promoted the game around the east coast, from his own estates next door to Carnoustie up to Montrose and Aberdeen.

The railway in 1847 linked up this whole area, from "Bonnie Dundee," a large trading and merchant town famous for jam, journalism and jute just 25 minutes from Carnoustie. The following year Allan Robertson and Tom Morris were invited over from St. Andrews to lay out an official 10 hole course for the Caledonian Union Club (supposedly made up of the best clubmen from St. Andrews, Perth and Montrose) and so the Taymouth Links and the Carnoustie and Taymouth Club came into existence. The Dalhousie Club was formed and another eight holes added in 1867. This was very much a family affair, as Tom Morris was responsible for this addition, his brother George supervised the construction as keeper of its greens, and Tom's son won the inaugural professional tournament, just sixteen years old. Young Tom went on to win three back-to-back Opens while still a teenager.

It is hardly surprising that Carnoustie didn't need to attract "the visitor," as they had so many home clubs and golfers of their own. The Union Club scrapped its elitism and became the Caladonian followed by the Carnoustie Mercantile and the New Taymouth!

This wealth of homegrown talent was to make its mark in America from around the turn of the century. Three Smiths made their mark in the

Moray Firth
Moray
Nairn
INVERNESS
Fraserburgh
Peterhead
Cruden Bay
Royal Aberdeen
ABERDEEN
Montrose
North Sea
Carnoustie
DUNDEE *Monifieth*
PERTH

The East Coast to the Moray Firth

CARNOUSTIE THE 6TH HOLE IS A 500 YARD PAR FIVE WITH AN OUT-OF-BOUNDS
TO THE LEFT AND CENTRALLY PLACED FAIRWAY BUNKERS. HOGAN'S ALLEY IS THE
NARROW GAP BETWEEN.

States as the popularity of the game spread. Will Smith lead the way by winning the U.S. Open with ease in 1899, having just emigrated to take up the newly appointed post of professional at Shinnecock Hills. Alex went one better, winning two Opens and coming home to play in the 1905 Championship at St. Andrews. Entered from the USA, Alex Smith was the first to represent America. The youngest brother, MacDonald Smith, came back on six occasions to compete in the Open, finishing third three years in a row when, on the last occasion at Prestwick in 1925 an unruly crowd got overexcited at the prospect of his winning and just didn't give him room to play. He took 83 in the last round and lost by three shots. Smith was runner-up to Jones at Hoylake during Jones' Grand Slam. Around 140 Carnoustie-reared men would become club professionals in the States by the time Bobby Jones won "The Slam" in 1930. Under the influence of yet another Carnoustie man, Stewart Maiden, Jones was taught and guided through his career by the Scot in East Lake, Atlanta.

Like most bunkers on the links of Scotland, most holes have names. I wonder how many there are called "Braid's Brawest" or "Lang Whang" (long drive) throughout the country? A tour of Carnousties starts at "Cup," on to "Gulley" and "Jockies Burn"—from the fourth, "Hillocks, Brae, and Long (now Hogans Alley) to Plantation , Short and Railway." From the turn, the 10th hole, "South America," is unexpected—it came about when a local caddie, after ten pints too many, announced to his colleagues that he was off to South America to seek his fortune. He was found asleep, using his suitcase as a pillow, by the 10th tee the next morning! On to "Dyke," (old stone wall) the eleventh, "Southward Ho, Whins, Spectacles, Luckyslap, Barry Burn, Island," and, finally, "Home."

The Carnoustie Opens.... "Six of the best!"

The year after the "Grand Slam," Carnoustie played host to the Open. James Braid carefully repositioned greens and tees, and, by adding well-placed bunkers, brought the course up to championship standard.

From that moment on it had, and still retains, the reputation of being the most demanding on the circuit—especially over its finishing holes. There have been six Open Championships played over the links in recent years. "The Silver Scot," Tommy Armour, so called for his prematuring grey hair, was the first winner in 1931. It was a popular victory locally, despite the fact that Armour was yet another who had left his home country permanently to seek fame and fortune, winning the U.S. Open in 1927. Englishman Henry Cotton withstood the challenge of the American Ryder Cup Team to win in waterlogged conditions on the last day in 1937. Ben Hogan bettered his score on every round, finishing with a 68 on his one and only visit to the Open, when winning in 1953. The length of Carnoustie, 7,252 yards, was the longest recorded for an Open Championship when Gary Player won in 1968. The South African described it as the most difficult course in the world! It was a tense affair that year with Jack Nicklaus never more than two shots behind. Tom Watson was victorious in the first of his five great Open wins after an 18-hole play-off against the luckless Australian Jack Newton in 1975. Again Nicklaus was in contention, one shot behind, along with fellow American Johnny Miller.

If the competitors and their followers had been told after Willie Auchterlonie's win at Prestwick in 1893 that there would not be another home-based Scot lifting the claret jug for 106 years, there would have been a stunned silence (to say the least), for it would have seemed incomprehensible to the dominant professionals of that era. Paul Lawrie triumphed after a "theatrical" finish from Frenchman Jean Van de Velde, who snatched defeat from the jaws of victory to allow a play-off at Carnoustie in 1999. The Scotsman, against all odds, broke that spell, or curse that had stayed with the Open since Auchterlonie's day.

CARNOUSTIE **ABOVE**: THE 8TH HOLE, A SHORT PAR 3, SEEMS TO OFFER A MOMENT'S RESPITE FROM THE RIGOURS OF NEGOTIATING YOUR WAY ROUND THIS DAUNTING CHAMPIONSHIP COURSE. **BELOW**: THE 13TH IS A PAR 3 WITH DRAMATIC BUNKERING BUT, THANKFULLY, HAS A GENEROUS GREEN TO PLAY TO.

Carnoustie is proof that it doesn't always take a dramatic site or beautiful surroundings for a great design to be fully appreciated. Its challenging bunkering is sure to effect the tact of one's play, as well as one's mental creativity as to how to get out of the bunker! Even though the course has been lengthened to allow for a difficult set up during The Open, it is still a very fair test and home of the 2nd most famous burn in the game of golf.

Carnoustie #14

The subtleties of this course abound, and the drive on the 14th is no exception. With gorse plants obscuring much of the fairway and bunkers refined to gobble up shots that stray off line, there is much more to this drive than meets the eye. Speaking of eye, the spectacle bunkers await on the second shot are the less subtle, but equally challenging issues faced on this short par 5. Brilliantly positioned, they encourage you to challenge them, as laying up in front of them leaves one with a 'blind' approach on the third shot.

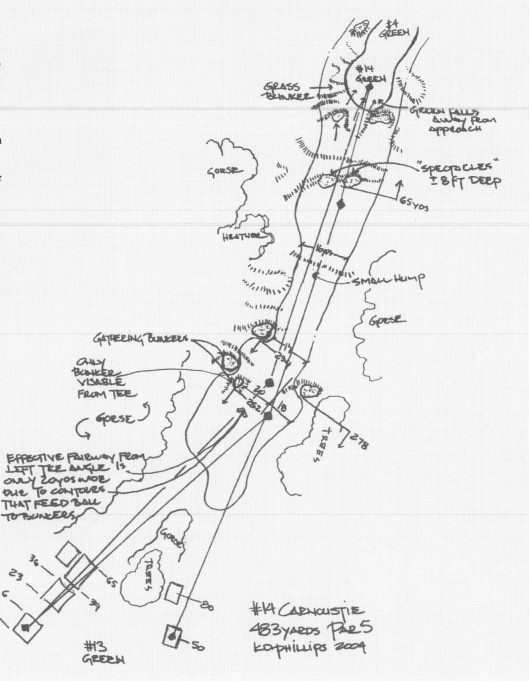

ABOVE: THE 14TH, A DOGLEG LEFT PAR 5, IS A VISU-
ALLY DRAMATIC HOLE AND DEEP SHADOWS FURTHER
EMPHASISE THE INTIMIDATING CHALLENGE. RIGHT:
LATE EVENING SUN HIGHLIGHTS THE CONTOURS ON
THIS LONG DOUBLE GREEN.

Scottish Golf Links

CARNOUSTIE THE 16TH, PAR 3, AT OVER 240 YARDS LONG, REQUIRES A VERY SOLID AND ACCURATE TEE SHOT. THE LONG UPHILL GREEN, PROTECTED BY BUNKERS FRONT LEFT AND RIGHT, RUNS OFF ON THREE SIDES.

PANMURE

A well-established club and course which, like Leven, Lundin Links, and Elie in "The Kingdom," shares a similar stretch of linksland with Monifeith and Carnoustie on the Angus coast. The club, established in 1845, still maintains the original spring and autumn meetings and dinners in the grand traditional manner. The Panmure Golf Club appropriately competed in the first "Grand Tournament" in 1857 in St. Andrews, when the 12 established clubs sent two members each to do battle against each other in two-ball foursomes. Blackheath, the only English club, won, but were represented by two Scotsmen who were also members of most of the other clubs—so everybody was happy! It was common at that time to be a member of at least three or four of the main clubs from the west coast to the east coast.

During the 1890s Panmure hosted many great exhibition matches with the triumvirate of Vardon, Taylor, and Braid taking on local heroes such as Jack Simpson, the 1884 Open Champion. Simpson from Carnoustie was the first to break the monopoly of the St. Andrews, Musselburgh, and Prestwick professionals in the Open. In fact, "The First Official Scottish Professionals Championship" was played at Panmure as late as 1907.

In 1931 the course was used for Open qualifying for Carnoustie as in 1968, '75 and '99 and for St. Andrews in 1970 and '90. Ben Hogan, the current U.S. and Masters Champion at that time, used the Panmure course and facilities in preparing himself for his masterful Carnoustie Open victory, when he quietly practiced the links shots he would need to manufacture a win. He even had his meals with the steward, unnoticed in the club's staff quarters. Hogan repeatedly played the sixth hole at Panmure from the tee, driving in a direct line over trouble—which he replicated on the same hole on the championship course, birdying it on the final two rounds. Brave shots, from which the hole has become known as "Hogan's Alley."

PANMURE   THE 3RD, PAR FOUR, IS OUT-OF-BOUNDS ON THE RIGHT AND HEAVILY BUNKERED DOWN THE LEFT.

PANMURE THE 6TH HOLE IS A SEMI-BLIND DOGLEG LEFT PAR 4.
IT WAS THE REQUIREMENT OF SUCH AN ACCURATE DRIVE THAT DREW
BEN HOGAN TO PRACTICE PRECISION ON THIS HOLE, PRIOR TO HIS WIN
AT CARNOUSTIE AND THE RESULTING NAMING OF "HOGANS ALLEY".

MONIFIETH

With the reputation of being a hard, uncompromising course, "The Medal" at Monifieth was the most difficult used in qualifying for the Carnoustie Open in 1975. Four clubs use the course, and have produced some fine amateurs in the modern game. The course dates from 1850, although records go back to the seventeenth century, as indeed they do for the whole of this coastline of Angus, Kincardineshire and Aberdeenshire. The railway line runs along the side of so many links courses, and Monifieth is no exception. Although initially a great asset for getting from one venue to the next, the railway claimed many parts of the ancient links that started and finished by the edge of their towns, with stations, goods, yards, and sidings taking over "the home holes."

MONIFIETH THE 10TH TEE TO GREEN, DOGLEG RIGHT.

MONIFIETH **ABOVE**: CLASSICAL TEXTURES OF THE APPROACH TO THE 16TH
GREEN. **OPPOSITE**: THE 9TH IS A 540 YARD PAR 5 AND BLIND FROM THE TEE.
I REVISITED THE COURSE IN JUNE 2004 AND THIS HOLE WAS PLAYING INTO A
THREE CLUB WIND!

Following the coast road from Carnoustie 20 miles north, past Arbroath (with yet another course over 100 years old,) is Montrose. It has glorious links that claim to be the fifth oldest in the world. Certainly one of the earliest records of the game originated from a student of St. Andrews University in 1574. He wrote in his diary that his father in Montrose had provided him with "glub an bals for goff but nocht a purss for catch pull and tavern" (club and ball for golf but nothing for hand tennis or drinking!). It is recorded that the famous, or infamous, Marquis of Montrose in 1629 played golf the night before his marriage and again immediately after the wedding ceremony!

From the book, British Golf Links 1896: "Once a Montrose man was asked at St. Andrews: "How do they golf at Montrose?" and, misunderstanding the question to refer to the methods rather than the calibre of the players, replied: "Oh they just hit at the ball and then swear." The course was well used by locals, as indicated by the clubs formed: The Royal Albert in 1813, The Mechanics in 1847, The Union in 1860, The Star in 1868, and The Victoria in 1870.

In 1785 a number of golfers in Montrose successfully presented a petition to the sheriffs to stop the town council allowing "grazing tenants" to plough or fence off part of the links. This was a reoccurring threat to links golf throughout the country until the Burgh Police Act in 1892 allowed compulsory purchase of public linksland by the towns. St. Andrews immediately safeguarded their rights through this Act and others followed suit.

Royal Montrose (so named when H.R.H. the Prince Consul Albert became its patron in 1845) is a wonderful example of true links. Sand hills or dunes created by sand blown from the beaches retain their shape with deep-rooted marram grass, which gave protection from strong winds and high tides. Erosion all the way along the coast, east and west, has been an ongoing problem for centuries. Pounding waves are quick to claim back any vulnerable hole near the shoreline as the first seven holes of Montrose will testify.

Tom Morris was called upon in 1901 to suggest reshaping, and Willie Park Jr., at the height of his career in course architecture, two years later adapted it, steering some holes away from the sea. The course survives and its image has been enhanced through the years. It was used in qualifying for the Carnoustie Open in 1999 for the first time. Like St. Andrews and Prestwick, Montrose conjures up images of the past where, through the constant sound of the sea, could be heard the "click" of an old ball by the swipe or "swoosh" of a whippy club.

ROYAL MONTROSE Looking back through the 4th green and fairway. Opposite: The 17th green, although without bunkers, is naturally protected by whin and a semi table top structure green.

ROYAL ABERDEEN 2ND GREEN AND UNDULATING FAIRWAY

ROYAL ABERDEEN **ABOVE**: THE 3RD GREEN TO TEE PAR 3.
BELOW: THE TEE, IN DANGER OF FALLING INTO THE SEA, GIVES ONLY
A PARTIAL VIEW OF THE 3RD GREEN.

ROYAL ABERDEEN

Forty miles further north lie the regal links of Aberdeen, which received patronage from Edward VII in 1915. The town council in 1565 branded golf as "an unlawful amusement" (but only if it interfered with dwindling attendances to sermons on the Sabbath!). There was enough interest in playing the game to merit John Dickson a permit from the council to exercise the trade of making golf balls for the community in the 1640s.

Just 20 years before, this was the first record anywhere in Scotland of "actual holes" being on a course. "The Hole" is the crucial factor in us Scots claiming the game as our own. Forget the Dutch and their game, *kolven*, or the French and their *jue de mail*, even the Romans with *paganica*…there was no hole! In the Aberdeen reference no indication of their size is mentioned, but then again they varied from a small hole scraped out with a knife, ending up the size of a Balmoral bonnet on a busy medal day! This was caused by scooping the earth or sand out of the hole by hand and creating a mound to tee off on, just a club length away. A wily member of the Society of Golfers at Aberdeen (founded in 1780) might well have applied for a late tee time in the hope of holing a few more putts as the size of the hole became more "sociable" on the way around.

The ancient links of Aberdeen along with those of Leith near Edinburgh had rough chartered maps of both their five-hole courses, which still survive to confirm their early existence.

The Society manfully tried to keep old traditions alive and were the last of the old clubs to wear a uniform—a red jacket with brass buttons and a black velvet cap. In 1887 this attire was abandoned as impracticable. Another major decision was made that year to move to new ground to the north of the River Don's estuary at Balgownie. The town's links, which they had played on for over 100 years, had become severely congested with locals exercising their rights to play football and cricket, to parade, and even to hang and dry their fishing nets on it!

ROYAL ABERDEEN THE 8TH, A SHORT PAR 3, HAS A FORTRESS OF BUNKERS SURROUNDING IT.

ROYAL ABERDEEN

An Architectural View by Kyle Phillips

Royal Aberdeen is one of the most spectacular natural sites in Scottish links golf, this is perhaps further emphasized due to the encroachment of the distant urban development of Aberdeen City. The opening hole plays directly towards the sea, the routing then turns directly along the shoreline and, playing inside the protection of high sand dunes, offers a variety of challenging holes that utilize all of the dramatic variation of nature's landscaping. Even though the back nine's return is further back from the sea, their elevated position offer sea views and continuing challenge. This is a venue worthy of far more recognition than it receives.

Royal Aberdeen #9

This long, difficult par 4 plays from an elevated tee at a diagonal across the natural dune landscape to a narrow fairway that leads back up to an elevated green. One must carefully judge distance and direction, while factoring in the anticipated influences of the breeze. The ideal drive lands in the short rough grass on the down slope, releasing into the center of the fairway. A drive played into the center of the fairway can easily go through into the rough when the conditions are fast and firm. Even when an ideal drive is achieved, there is no relief on the long approach to the green where any shot struck less than perfectly is likely to find the guarding bunkers or long rough surrounding the green.

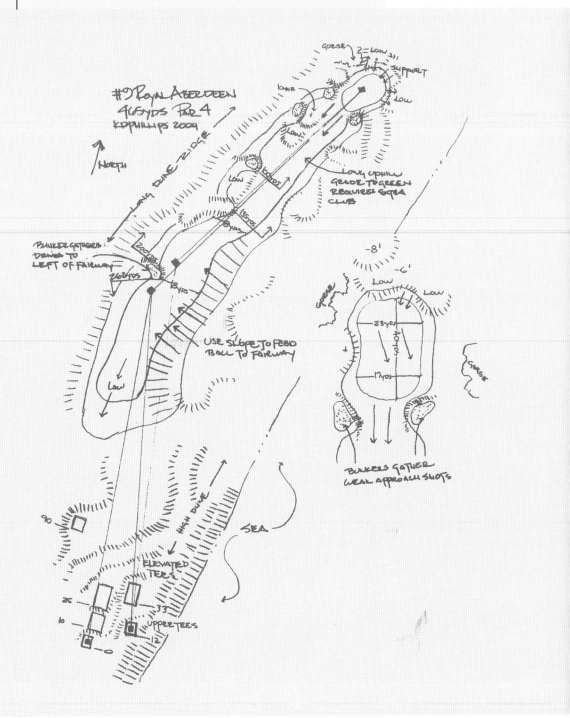

THE VIEW FROM THE 9TH TEE ACROSS A BROAD
EXPANSE OF DUNES AND LONG GRASSES GIVES ONLY A
HINT OF A FLAG IN THE DISTANCE. THE HEAVILY SHAD-
OWED FAIRWAY AND THE AERIAL VIEW COMBINE TO
ENHANCE THE BEAUTY AND CHALLENGE OF THIS HOLE.

ROYAL ABERDEEN **OPPOSITE:** THE 17TH IS A HEAVILY
BUNKERED DOWNHILL PAR 3 AND VERY OPEN TO THE SEA BREEZES.
BELOW: THE FINAL HOLE, ILLUMINATED BY GORSE IN THE SPRING-
TIME AND THE BLOOM OF HEATHER IN THE LATE SUMMER.

MURCAR

Murcar is as fine a links course as you could wish to play," said the 1999 Open Champion Paul Lawrie. He learned the game and played around the northeast courses from a young age. The Murcar links run close to Royal Aberdeen when it brushes past the 10th tee on Aberdeen's homeward trek back toward the town. Established in 1909, the layout was supervised by Archie Simpson, who held the course record of 71 on the Royal course. Simpson advertised himself as a "Professional golf player, Balgownie Links, Aberdeen. Maker of best golf clubs and balls. Professional advice given in laying out new golf courses." Almost inevitably, James Braid had a hand in turning Murcar into a challenging test of golf, which is frequently credited in the top 100 courses of the British Isles. Peter Alliss, in a much overused phrase, but true in this case, described it as "a hidden gem."

MURCAR **Opposite:** The burn cutting through the centre of a rolling fairway, makes the 7th tee and uphill approach shot difficult to negotiate. **Above:** The 3rd green borders the 10th tee of Royal Aberdeen.

CRUDEN BAY THE SUN, LOW IN THE SKY, EMPHASISES
THE LINKSLAND OF CRUDEN BAY. TO THE LEFT THE 6TH
HOLE "BLUIDY BURN" WITH THE 17TH BOTTOM RIGHT.
TUCKED INTO THE DUNES ABOVE CAN BE SEEN THE 7TH
AND 16TH GREENS.

CRUDEN BAY

The clubhouse here has one of the best bird's-eye views—it gives the impression of the links being a course architect's model. Flanked by its bay, it stretches north to the sinister ruin of Slains Castle perched up on a cliff. Bram Stoker developed the character Count Dracula here in 1893. The Cruden Bay course has quite a different look about it when you get down to play and attempt to steer the ball through its towering dunes. It must have appeared an easy task initially, to the eccentric Englishman Tom Simpson when commissioned to revamp the course in 1926—as he could see everything before him!

Originally set up by the Great North of Scotland Railway Company as part of a leisure complex in 1898—the ploy was to encourage holiday-makers to use their luxurious Great North of Scotland Railway Hotels. It did well at first but the Depression of the early 30s marked a rapid decline in the viability of keeping on the once regal Cruden Bay Hotel. It had originally promoted itself and attracted many visitors as "A health resort with sandy beaches and an excellent golf course with extensive links."

Tom Morris was asked to create a course that would attract visitors from afar. On such a unique and quirky piece of linksland he took full advantage of its natural but unpredictable terrain and threaded his way through all its eccentricities. Archie Simpson contributed to its initial design with frequent visits, and by April 1899 the links was ready for an inaugural professional tournament. The end result was, and still is, memorable, fun, and at times very demanding. Harry Vardon won that first competition, attracting a huge crowd as the then Open Champion. (He successfully defended his title later that year at Sandwich.)

Bernard Darwin, the noted golf writer, describing some of the holes of Cruden Bay when it opened, said "Some of the shots are blind—wilfully blind if you like to call it so…but there are also some truly fine golfing holes, on the grand scale." In more recent times, American course architect Pete Dye described Cruden Bay as "outsized, nonconformist, unpredictable, flamboyant—certainly among the top 10 courses of Scotland that on no account should be missed."

CRUDEN BAY THE 5TH, SKIRTS AROUND AND OVER THE DUNES AS A DOGLEG LEFT PAR 4.

The routing of the course is masterful, taking full advantage of the variety that the natural site has to offer. Playing along the base of an ancient sea cliff, through some of the most impressive sand dunes and along the edge of the sea, Cruden Bay is a delight to play and isn't this after all the true measure of a successful design?

Cruden Bay #6

Even though the way this hole plays has changed from the days its design was conceived, the design of this short par 5 is still relevant for today's best players.

An exhilarating driving hole from an elevated tee to a spacious fairway below, this hole rewards the long driver with a very realistic opportunity to attack this elevated green, situated just over the burn, on their second shot. However, an errant drive into the rough, particularly down the left, will be cause to lay up short of the burn in two.

One of the unique features of the design of this hole is the bunkers and series of small moguls in the area just short of the burn. These, coupled with the steep dune down the left, make lying up on the second shot a work of precision. In fact, many players will contemplate lying back just in front of the sand bunkers.

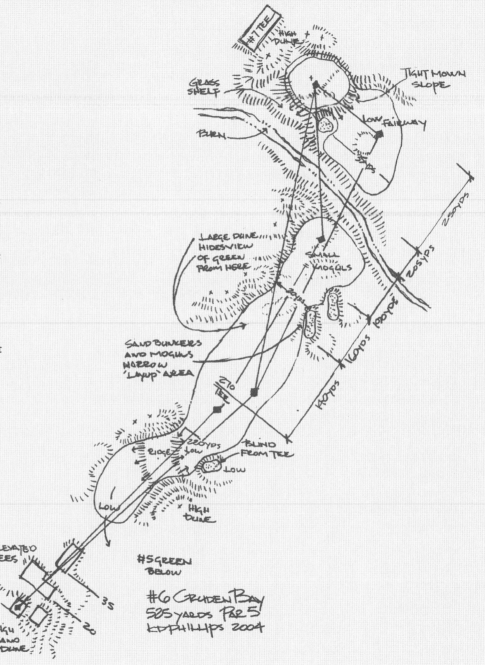

T THE "BLUIDY BURN", PROTECTS THE FRONT OF THE ELEVATED
6TH GREEN SET IN THE MIDST OF TOWERING DUNES.

CRUDEN BAY OPPOSITE: THIS ELEVATED VIEW OF THE 11TH TEE TO ITS RAISED
GREEN, HIGHLIGHTS FEARSOME BUNKERING AND SHOWS THE PATH OF THE BURN MAK-
ING ITS WAY TO THE SEA. ABOVE: THE CLASSIC VIEW OF CRUDEN BAY TAKEN FROM
ABOVE THE 16TH TEE LOOKING TOWARDS ITS GREEN, CENTRE STAGE. TO THE RIGHT
THE 15TH GREEN, AND TO THE LEFT THE WHITE FLAG SIGNALS THE 7TH GREEN.

CRUDEN BAY IN THE MIDDLE OF THE 17TH FAIRWAY, THE SHADOW OF A 15 FOOT HIGH MOUND GIVES INDICATION OF THE DIFFICULTY THAT MAY OCCUR TO THE APPROACH OF ITS TABLE TOP GREEN. **OPPOSITE**: THIS VIEW FROM THE CLUBHOUSE OF THE 18TH AND TO THE DISTANT 6TH GREEN IS THE SETTING THAT MAKES CRUDEN BAY SO DISTINCTIVE IN THE TOUR OF LINKS COURSES.

CRUDEN BAY A PASSING STORM LEAVES A HEAVY FALL OF SNOW ON
THE 15TH WINTER GREEN AND BUNKER. ACROSS THE BAY THE LATE SUN
HIGHLIGHTS THE CLIFFTOP AND RUINS OF SLANE CASTLE.

PETERHEAD

O n just about the most northerly point of Aberdeenshire's east
coast, just a few miles up from Cruden Bay, lies the busy fishing
port of Peterhead. The links, partly exposed to the relentless
force of the North Sea, has had a real problem stemming the tide of coastal
erosion, even as recently as the 1960s. When the Peterhead Golf Club was
formed in 1841 the members played away on just four holes (three times
made a round) along the edge of the vulnerable dunes of Cairntrodlie.

Willie Park Jr., who was to become known as the "doyen" of golf
architects, was invited to lay out a nine-hole course when new ground was
acquired at Craigwan Links in 1892. He shaped the new Peterhead links,
starting with the first hole using the contour of the bank of the River Ugie.
Park took the ditches, tracks, water hazards and potential out-of-bounds
ground and put them to good use. His business built up very quickly, and
after constructing the prestigious Sunningdale course in England, Park set
off in 1908 to build or remodel over 70 courses in North America in a prolific period of course design up to 1925.

In the same year that Park went over the sea, the Peterhead club
secured more ground and another nine holes were added. Even more land
was leased in 1923 and another course put in place. In 1929 James Braid
visited to advise the club on bunkering (87 of them in play today) and
improving their new course. Today, a modern new clubhouse stands impe-
riously looking out over all the past club committees' and individuals'
endeavours in securing the Craigwan Links at Peterhead.

PETERHEAD **ABOVE:** LOOKING BACK THROUGH THE 7TH GREEN TO THE OPENING
HOLES. **BELOW:** FROM THE 8TH TEE EARLY MORNING LIGHT SHOWS THE BEAUTY OF
A ROLLING LINKS COURSE THROUGH THE 16TH AND 10TH GREENS — TO PETERHEAD
AND ACROSS ITS BAY.

Round to the Moray Firth

Moving around to the north coast is a line of fishing villages, large and small. Old Tom Morris had spent time travelling back and forth from St. Andrews in the early 1890s laying out and advising on courses along this stretch. Moving west from Fraserburgh, into Bannfshire and Duff House Royal at Banff where in 1637 Franceis Broun was hanged for stealing golf balls! Cullen, the next course in line, takes you on to Lossiemouth, Forres, and Nairn on the east side of the Moray Firth.

There are plenty references to golf in all its shapes and forms in this area—from "short" (putting) and "long" golf, to challenge matches between the landed gentry and village or town matches. For example: *The Golfing Annual 1887*, in an extract after describing Fraserburgh Links:

"As some indication of the estimation in which the game is held, it may be mentioned that thirty or forty years back New Year's Day was entirely devoted to golfing, and on that occasion a large number of the natives of the adjacent fishing villages—no mean players in their day—met a selected team of the inhabitants on the links of Fraserburgh to do battle for a fixed sum of money. On completion of the match, victors and vanquished adjourned to the leading ale-house, where the sum at stake was duly consumed in liquor, and the match 'played over again,' at times in the most uproarious manner. Although a period of lethargy ensued, golfing has in recent years made great progress"

But all was not well as this brief report on Banff in the same book records, "No interest being taken by the townspeople, the club is in a morbid condition, which is a pity as the links are pretty, and much could be made of them."

Some 200 years earlier, "Ife ye have a mind for a touch at the long gauff tomorrow lett mee know" was a message from James Ogilvie in Banff, sent to his cousin along the road at Cullen where they were playing in 1690. "This is not that I doubt that ye mak good use of your short putting club here," he said, suggesting the greens were in good order!

CULLEN, PART CLIFFTOP AND PART SEASIDE, HAS SOME DRAMATIC FREE-STANDING ROCKS TO PLAY OVER AND AROUND.

LOSSIEMOUTH A LONG VIEW OF THE BUNKER PROTECTED 1ST HOLE (LEFT) AND THE 17TH GREEN (RIGHT) SHOWING THE SWEEP OF DUNES THAT PROTECT THE OPENING AND CLOSING HOLES. **OPPOSITE**: THE ELEVATED 18TH GREEN WITH ITS TRADITIONAL CLUBHOUSE BACKDROP.

MORAY, LOSSIEMOUTH

Old Tom Morris laid out "The Old Course" in 1889. It is in fact similar to its namesake in St. Andrews as the first seven holes run straight out from the town—round a loop and back in again. The sound of jets on exercise from nearby RAF Lossiemouth, can also be heard from RAF Leuchars over the links of St. Andrews. Another comparison is that, like Morris's New Course in his hometown, the Moray course has stood the test of time, with very little change apart from the lengthening of it. It retains the unpredictable bounce on bone hard summer links fairways.

Like Muirfield, you get what you see without a blind shot on the course. Fifteen par 4s (10 over 400 yards), two fives, and a three make up this classic links of 6,643 yards, with a par of 73.

The Moray Golf Club expelled one of its local members, Ramsay McDonald, for his outspoken pacifist views during the First World War. When he became Prime Minister in 1924 the committee was called to reconsider his membership—he was outvoted!

Still on the east of the Moray Firth, the links of the Nairn Golf Club run along its side. The firth narrows to about 10 miles in width with "The Black Isle" looming on its far bank. Like so many Scottish courses of note, it was laid out by Tom Morris and reworked later by James Braid on three separate occasions from 1910 up to 1926. Having set a course record there in 1902, Braid was familiar and fond of this exceptional links and often said that it accommodated the best turf and greens in the land.

As far back as 1797 the town council allowed the growing and sale of this much-sought-after grass (nurtured on a base of white sand)—as long as it didn't interfere with the gowf! Wild grass, to establish itself, had to be tough and versatile to survive against moving sand, drought, and frost. Because of this, it was slow growing and springy—with a little help from sheep and rabbits to cut and fertilise, it was ideal for the game of golf.

It was an ambitious and formidable group that set up the course and officially formed the Nairn Golf Club in 1887. The Right Hon. Earl Cawdor was its president, backed up by his vice presidents, which included Major Rose of Kilravock Solicitor–General; Colonel Clarke of Achareidh; Sir Robert Finlay Q.C. M.P. of Newton; and General MacDonnell. Within 10 years major structural changes had been made to the links, a ladies course added, and a major competition hosted. Most of the membership of 450 with their wives and guests would have seen Laurie Auchterlonie from St. Andrews lift the £100 purse and a handsome trophy in the 1895 tournament, open to amateurs and professionals. Auchterlonie went on to win the U.S. Open in 1902.

Nairn's picturesque surroundings with that fine sweep of the bay, and the Ross-shire range of hills with Ben Wyvis as its centerpiece, had visitors flock to the area in its traditionally short summer season. With the Gulf Stream curling around the northeast corner into the Moray Firth, winter play for the locals was more or less uninterrupted. It was claimed that snow was never said to lie on the course, although the resident professional, James Dalgleish, always kept a substantial supply of red balls in the clubhouse. In 1897, asked why he had so many if it never snowed up there, he replied that it was because there had never been an occasion to use or lose any of them!

Dalgleish joined the rank of golfing immigrants in the States; based in Kansas, he designed and laid out courses in Missouri and Minnesota.

Like Dornoch, the Nairn links has attracted international editorial press in major golf magazines over recent years. It hosted the British Amateur Championship in 1994 and continues to grow in reputation.

NAIRN CLASSIC LINKS TEXTURES AND COLOURS OF THE 4TH HOLE COMBINE WITH THE BACKDROP OF THE MORAY FIRTH TO MAKE A GREAT PAR 3.

NAIRN **ABOVE**: APPROACH TO THE PAR FIVE 10TH HOLE. **RIGHT**: A TEE TO GREEN
VIEW OF THE DOWNHILL 14TH **OPPOSITE**: A BRILLIANT, CLEAR BLUE SKY AND LATE
AFTERNOON SUN ADDS WARMTH TO THE PAR 5 18TH GREEN AND CLUBHOUSE.

Scottish Golf Links

Leaving Nairn, just 15 miles down the road awaits the highland capital city of Inverness, where the waters of Loch Ness flow into the Moray Firth. To points further north and 50 miles to Dornoch, meandering through the Black Isle to Easter Ross. Passing the sheltered west bank of the Cromarty Firth, redundant and travel-weary semi-submersible oil rigs float incongruously, unexpectedly, on the way to more memorable links courses.

ROYAL DORNOCH Brilliant yellow blooms surround the 4th, 5th and 6th holes. The low, late evening, sunset casts its luminous shadow across familiar bunkers and greens.

The Links of Dornoch in the early seventeenth century were said to be equal to St. Andrews for golf and archery and compared favourably with Montrose, Leith, and Musselburgh as a venue for race meetings—"horses for courses!" This is backed up by Sir Robert Gordon, tutor to the young Earl of Sutherland in 1616, who wrote that along the seacoast at Dornoch were the fairest and largest links or green fields of any part of Scotland.

In 1877 the Dornoch club was formed with the encouragement of Alexander McHardy, known as "the Pioneer of Golf in Northern Scotland," and Dr. Hugh Gunn, a graduate of St. Andrews University. An official nine-hole course had been constructed, and in 1883 John Sutherland (aptly named) became its secretary, a position he would hold for 50 years. Like Tom Morris and St. Andrews, Charlie Hunter and Prestwick, Sutherland became synonymous with Dornoch. His reputation and knowledge of the game was such that he was invited to write for *Golf Illustrated* and the *London Daily News* at the turn of the century—which helped profile and publicise the town and its links. He had made a big impact, for within two years of becoming secretary, Sutherland had invited Morris up and 18 holes were in play by 1886. Morris was said to be "charmed" by the links, saying, as many have since, that there was no better to be found for golf. He was particularly impressed with the numerous small plateau, or table hillocks, some of which he utilised and converted into square greens!

The railway was late in arriving at Dornoch, but when it did connect in 1902, suddenly it seemed to be the most desirable of locations. Making use of the sleeping car service from London to Inverness was a fashionable

The North Coast

THE IMPRESSIVE OPENING HOLE, SET WITH TACTICALLY PLACED POT BUNKERS.

thing to do, and so an influx of folk with status and wealth arrived in town, despite the length of the journey. Cheap fares for golfers "to the splendid links of Dornoch and Nairn" were advertised by the Highland Railway, encouraging a direct route from St. Andrews via Perth and Inverness.

Donald Ross

Local man Donald Ross, who was to become a famous name in course architecture in the States, fell under the influence of Morris. As an accomplished golfer and with the encouragement of John Sutherland, he left Dornoch to learn the art of club making with Forgans in St. Andrews. Tom Morris took Ross under his wing in an extensive period of course design as "the grand old man" toured the country. The young Ross watched and assisted in many courses being laid out in Scotland, England, and Ireland in three years from 1890. He went back to Dornoch as greenskeeper and put his experiences to good use before being lured away to Boston at the turn of the century. His brother Alex, who had been his assistant in the club-maker's shop, went with him and won the U.S. Open in 1907. Donald Ross became a prolific course designer and at one point in 1925 had over 3,000 men gainfully employed in his constructions. Morris and the Dornoch influence shone through in the way he constructed his most famous course: Number Two at Pinehurst in North Carolina.

ROYAL DORNOCH LEFT: IF YOUR TEE SHOT ON THE 2ND HOLE DOES NOT HOLD THE GREEN, THE SECOND SHOT ON THIS DIFFICULT PAR 3 HAS THE POTENTIAL OF BEING THE MOST CHALLENGING RECOVERY SHOT YOU WILL EVER HAVE TO FACE. ABOVE: THE IVY-COVERED BIRTHPLACE OF DONALD ROSS.

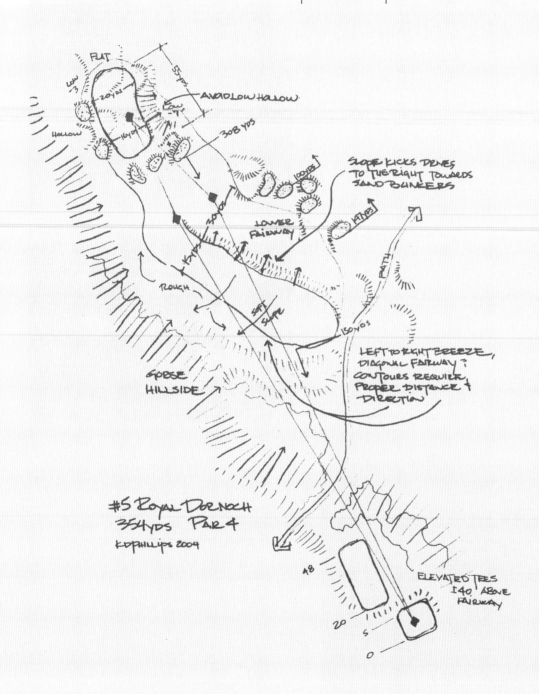

Because of the geology of the site, similar to that of Kingsbarns, the course offers some of the best sea views in links golf. The trade-off is that it is not as easy to walk as some of the low lying links courses. The routing uses the terrain and the change of angles provides great variety in the effects of the wind. The greens, particularly on the first six holes, offer subtle borrows that can punish the unwary.

Royal Dornoch #5

One of the most fun short par 4's in Scotland. The elevated tee, wide fairway and softly contoured elevated green give hope for a birdie. Those that choose to lie back from the tee must avoid the ridge that runs down the middle of the fairway and pulls shots toward the nest of fairway bunkers on the right. But when the conditions are firm, long drives can leave delicate approach shots that must avoid being swept down the long, tightly mown slope on the right.

RIGHT: THE ELEVATED 5TH TEE ALLOWS A CLEAR VIEW OF
ALL THAT PUNISHES ANY WAYWARD DRIVE ON THIS SHORT
PAR 4. BELOW: BUNKERS LINE THE RIGHT SIDE OF THE FAIR-
WAY AND PROTECT THE FRONT OF THIS ELEVATED GREEN.

A CLEAR VIEW OF THE 5TH GREEN BACK TO THE TEE
WITH THE PANORAMA OF THE COURSE, WHICH HAS
ENHANCED THE REPUTATION OF ROYAL DORNOCH.

ROYAL DORNOCH **ABOVE**: TWO EXTREME SEASONAL VIEWS OF THE 5TH AND 11TH GREENS. **OPPOSITE**: THE 14TH, "FOXY", HAS NO BUNKERS BUT IS RECOGNISED AS A MOST DEMANDING PAR 4. THE RIGHT SIDE OF THE FAIRWAY HAS DOMINATING RIDGES OF VARIOUS PROTRUDING SHAPES AND SIZES AND A GREEN AT RIGHT ANGLES TO IT.

Scottish Golf Links

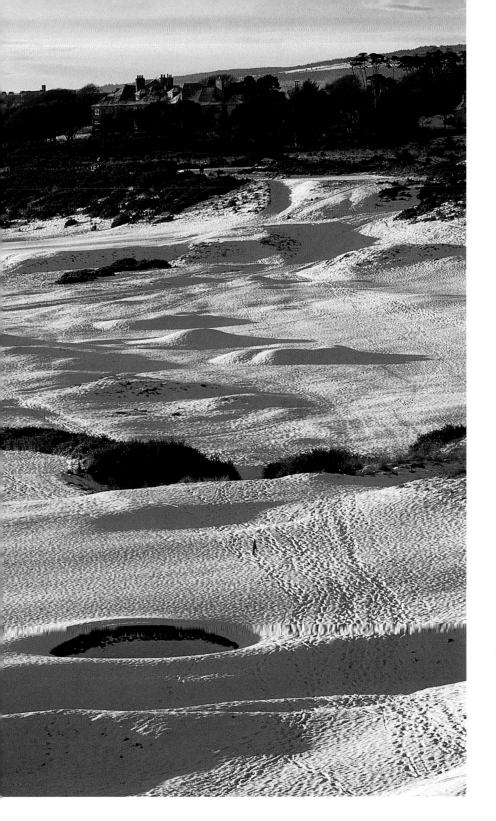

ROYAL DORNOCH PRIDES ITSELF FOR BEING OPEN ALL YEAR ROUND WITH SNOW A RARE OCCASIONAL VISITOR. WHEN IT DOES LIE, THE LATE EVENING SUN CASTS A RICH COLOUR THAT ADDS BEAUTY AND ATMOSPHERE TO THIS MOST NORTHERLY CHAMPIONSHIP COURSE.

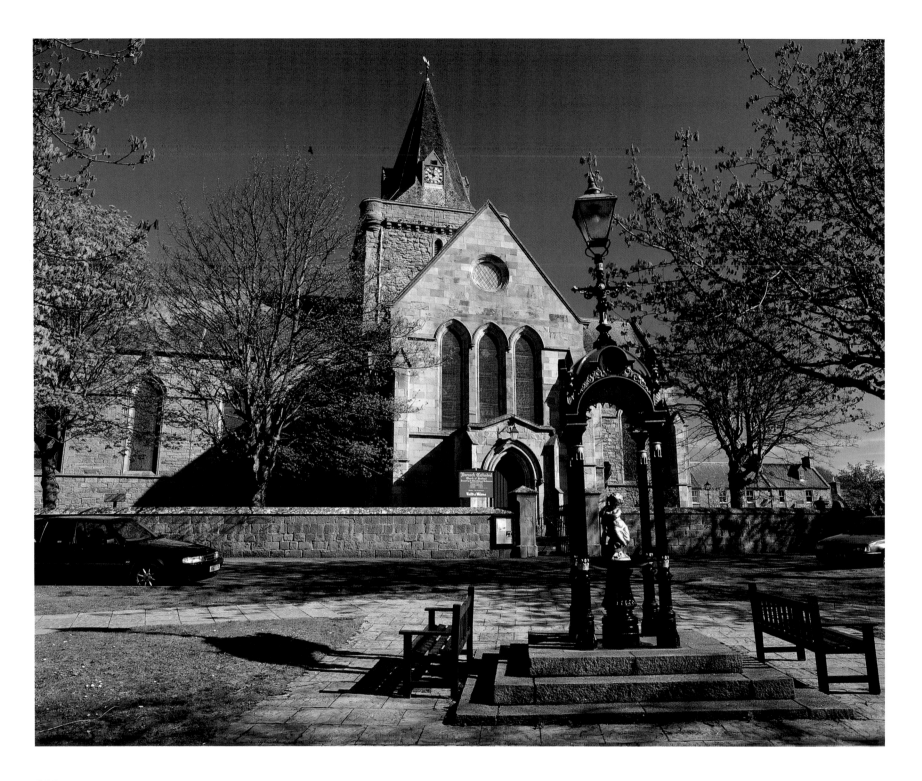

Carnegie and the Cathedral

Andrew Carnegie, a Scotsman who had made his fortune in America as a steel magnate and philanthropist, spent a fortune rebuilding Skibo Castle, four miles along the Firth and turned it into one of the world's great residences. In its grounds he had John Sutherland lay out a private course. As vice president, Carnegie presented a shield to the Dornoch club at the opening of its new clubhouse in 1909. The trophy, still played for in competition today, has skillfully engraved illustrations of Dornoch Cathedral in silver as its centerpiece. This was most appropriate because, like St. Andrews, the town grew through the years and life revolved around its medieval cathedral—noted for its first service in the thirteenth century and for its influential golfing clergy of the seventeenth century, among other events of note: pop star Madonna's much-publicised wedding at the beginning of this century!

Back in 1906 King Edward VII granted a Royal Charter to Dornoch Golf Club. He had been a frequent visitor and often stayed with his friend the Duke of Sutherland in Dunrobin Castle near the links of Brora, or with Carnegie at Skibo.

The triumvirate of Vardon, Taylor, and Braid were unanimous in their praise for the links. People took notice of their comments as, between them, 16 Open Championships had been won during a dominant period of 20 years from 1894. So impressed was J.H. Taylor that he chose to spend a two week holiday each year in Dornoch during the height of his career.

One hundred years later, five-time winner of the Open Tom Watson is equally lavish in his praise for Royal Dornoch. Had it not been so far "off the beaten track" it might well have hosted the Open Championship by now.

OPPOSITE: THE STATELY CATHEDRAL IN HIGH SUMMER AND ON A WINTERS NIGHT (RIGHT). ABOVE: THE BEAUTIFULLY HAND ENGRAVED CARNEGIE SHIELD.

Scottish Golf Links

Before crossing the Dornoch Firth lies the town of Tain looking out onto the Whiteness Sands. It is better known for its whisky distillery Glenmorangie, meaning "glen of tranquility." When its first keg was opened and the amber nectar bottled, it was dedicated, with great celebration, to St. Duffus, the patron saint of the town and club!

The links one mile to the east of Tain was originally a 12-hole course laid out by Tom Morris in 1890. Described in *The Golfing Annual of 1896* as "one that shows its thoroughly sporting nature, is the fact that only two holes can be seen from the tee as the players drive towards them, while in the case of six of them, the flag remains invisible until the player comes well within reach of the disc." Liberally supplied with whin, bent, and bunkers, Tain has a bit of Prestwick and "The Alps," with reminders of St. Andrews and Nairn along its run of holes by the sands—in fact, you could say, to flatter, that it is a compilation of "Tom Morris's greatest hits!"

In 1913 the Tain Golf Club bought a horse to pull a fairway mower. Shoes with wooden platforms tied into canvas bags and onto the hooves were used to prevent the turf being damaged. In the 1920s the treasurer worked out that it had cost £65 a year to keep and feed their horse with a work expectancy of about 10 years. A tractor would cost £55 and be less bother, and so the horse was "put out to grass" (made redundant) as greenskeeping equipment became more reliable and cost-effective.

TAIN **Opposite:** The approach to the 1st green at Tain requires a flick over a road and fence! **Right:** Although you may see the flag from the tee, by the time you play the approach "The Alps" will be a blind shot, so take note of the pin position from the board.

THE GLENMORANGIE WHISKY DISTILLERY, ON THE OUTSKIRTS OF TAIN, IS OPEN TO THE PUBLIC AND OFFERS AN INSIGHT INTO THE MAKING OF SCOTLAND'S FAMOUS DRAM. OPPOSITE: THE 17TH IS THE LAST PAR THREE AT TAIN WHERE A BURN HAS THE CHANCE TO CATCH YOUR BALL THIS WAY AND THAT.

GOLSPIE

This course has trees on it! Founded just two years after its near neighbour Dornoch in 1889, it is a mixture of heath, parkland, and links with ever-changing views, looking one way across the firth, and turning around to the northern highlands and Ben Bhraggie. Its four holes that run close to the sea have been vulnerable in the past. After a sandstorm buried the fourth hole in 1901, steps were taken in what has become a constant battle to prevent coastal erosion all the way around the east coast, from Dunbar to Durness.

GOLSPIE **OPPOSITE**: THE 3RD, 4TH AND 5TH HOLES PLAY ALONG A COASTLINE PROTECTED FROM THE CONTINUOUS BATTLE AGAINST EROSION. **BELOW**: VIEW FROM SHORT 16TH TEE TO THE GREEN PROTECTED BY A TWO TIER GREEN.

BRORA STANDING ON THE 1ST TEE, SURROUNDED BY THE RUGGED BEAUTY OF YET ANOTHER STRIKING NATURAL LINKS, A BIG HITTER MAY BE DECEIVED INTO GOING GO FOR THE GREEN JUST 280 YARDS DISTANT. BUT THE GREEN IS MOST UN-RECEPTIVE WHEN PLAYED FROM THIS DIRECTION AND THE AREA AROUND IT MOST INHOSPITABLE.

BRORA

Past the spectacular Dunrobin Castle between Golspie and Brora another links creeps north in a chain reaction of courses built around 1890. Tom Morris was involved yet again in laying out the original nine holes. In 1923 James Braid made the long journey by train from London, and in a day, masterfully sketched out what is now known as "Braid's Plan." He promptly caught the next train back down south, but his brief visit and fee of £25 was well worth it to the club who took on board all of Braid's recommendations. The result was an impressive reconstruction, which has hardly altered since. The James Braid Golfing Society meet in Brora every year, in appreciation of all the great golfer's and architect's achievements.

Watch where you step because there are cattle about the links. You may not be allowed a free drop on the fairways—but the cows are! There are also electric fences around the greens to discourage sheep or cattle from straying onto the putting surfaces!

BRORA **ABOVE**: THE IMPOSING DUNROBIN CASTLE. **BELOW**: THE GREENS ARE RINGED BY ELECTRIC FENCES TO KEEP CATTLE AND SHEEP AT BAY.

BRORA THIS ELEVATED POSITION SHOWS THE UNDULATING 17TH
FAIRWAY AND RAISED GREEN WITH THE FLAG STRAINING IN THE WIND.
THE LONG PAR 4 CAPTURES MUCH OF THE CHARM AND CHALLENGE OF
THIS SIGNATURE JAMES BRAID COURSE.

BRORA LOOKING BACK DOWN THROUGH THE 18TH GREEN, WITH A DEEP PRO-
TECTIVE VALLEY, AND OUT TO THE COAST WITH WAVES, MORE OFTEN THAN NOT,
CRASHING ONTO THE BEACH.

DURNESS THE MOST NORTHERLY GOLF COURSE IN SCOTLAND.

The trek to the furthest point north by Cape Wrath and the wonderful
Durness nine-hole course (which has two sets of tees to complete 18 holes)
is well worth the effort. Although a relatively new course design, it was
acknowledged in *The Golfing Illustrated Guide* of 1905 as an established
course. Also featured in the guide are Wick and Thurso with significant
courses over 100 years old, on the road up and along this dramatic coastline.

Before heading back to the start of the Scottish East Coast Trail of links courses at Dunbar (via Muirfield and North Berwick) there's a chance to experience the hills and the glens of central Scotland, from Inverness to Aviemore where the Grampian Mountains loom high — through Glen Garry to Pitlochry, following the banks of the River Tay to Perth. James VI learned to play golf there before acceding to the English throne in 1603 in the union of the crowns. The Royal Perth Golfing Society was formed in 1833, and many of the early challenge and professional tournaments were played at the North Inch in the 1860s.

Scottish Golf Links

TO GLENEAGLES

The Caledonian Railway Company decided in 1912 to build an opulent hotel with two courses —"a his and hers," in central Perthshire.

James Braid designed the Kings and Queens Courses, which were in play five years before the ambitious construction of the hotel. It became a world-class resort, surrounded by rolling hills and big dramatic views where eagles soar, in the heartland of Scotland. Prior to the Open Championship at St. Andrews in 1921, Gleneagles hosted a professional international match between Great Britain and the United States. It was to be the forerunner to the first Ryder Cup held in Worcester, Massachussets in 1927. Gleneagles accommodates this prestigious event in the year 2014 and is well geared up for it, having held the Bells Scottish Open and the McDonalds WPGA European Championship there in recent years.

The Monarchs, renamed the Centenary Course, was designed by Jack Nicklaus in 1993 and is complemented by the facility of a Golf Academy just before you step onto the first tee. It can be a demanding course to play but that ever-changing view across the Ochil Hills to the Grampians beyond will take your mind off bogeys and double bogeys.

THERE IS NO MISTAKING THE LOCATION OF GLENEAGLES, FROM ITS GRAND 1920'S DESIGNED HOTEL AND FORMAL GARDENS. THIS REGAL SCOTTISH HIGHLAND AND COUNTRY RETREAT OFFERS THREE COURSES AND MORE BESIDES.

GLENEAGLES KINGS COURSE 14TH GREEN A 300 YARD PAR FOUR. **BELOW**: LOOKING THROUGH THE SIDE OF THE QUEENS14TH GREEN TO THE 15TH TEE AND GREEN BEYOND. **OPPOSITE**: THE PGA CENTENARY COURSE APPROACH TO THE 1ST GREEN ENHANCED BY SPLENDOUR OF ITS HIGHLAND BACKDROP.

EDINBURGH *The Capital City*

From Gleneagles to Stirling past the ancient "park" in the shadow of it's 600 year-old castle. Where Royals played their "gowf" in the sixteenth century on heavy pasture not really suited for the game. Thirty five miles further down the road is Edinburgh. Known as "Auld Reekie" for the amount of smoke accumulated on it's skyline from row upon row of chimney pots burning coal and peat in the old part of the town. After the Union of the parliaments of 1707 the importance of the huge garrison housed in Edinburgh Castle declined and life became more settled and safe. This encouraged more recreation and leisure within the burgess society; bow makers turned their attention to making golf clubs and hostelries or inns were used as golf clubhouses up until the mid-1850's. It is claimed that the links of Leith, by the docklands of Edinburgh, having been played on for at least 200 years before the Union, are the oldest in the history of the game.

ABOVE: EDINBURGH CASTLE IS PERCHED HIGH ABOVE PRINCESS STREET.
LEFT AND OPPOSITE: CENTRAL EDINBURGH ABOUNDS WITH HISTORIC BUILDINGS, STATUES, MUSEUMS AND ART GALLERIES AND YET, WITH THE FRINGE FESTIVAL, THE EDINBURGH TATTOO AND NEW YEAR CELEBRATIONS, IS A CITY OF THE 21ST CENTURY.

MUIRFIELD THE APPROACH TO THE 11TH, FROM
A BLIND TEE SHOT, THIS GREEN, SET AGAINST A WIND
WHIPPED FIRTH OF FORTH, IS RINGED BY BUNKERS.

Musselburgh and its old nine-hole Open Championship course is the nearest to Edinburgh on the East Lothian Coast. Because of its proximity, the distinguished Edinburgh clubs moved over to play and share the links. Not surprisingly, it became over-loaded as a public course when it was accommodating the Honourable Company of Edinburgh Golfers, the Bruntsfield Links Golfing Society, the Edinburgh Burgesses, and the Royal Musselburgh Club at the same time!

Willie Park, the first Open Champion in 1860, was raised here and went on to win four championships. His brother Mungo won the first Musselburgh Open in 1874 and his son, who is frequently mentioned in this book for his course design, also won the great tournament in 1887 and '89. Sadly, Musselburgh is now better known for its racetrack and modern facilities surrounding the course, but is still acknowledged as having made a major contribution to the folklore and history of the game.

Farther down the coast, within a radius of two miles from Muirfield are five fine links courses that have all played their part in the history of the game. There was a friendly but competitive rivalry between the East Lothian clubs as they all participated annually for a County Cup, presented in 1864.

Following the landmarks (although out at sea), the islands of Fidra and Craigleith and the mighty Bass Rock with its colony of gannets take you to North Berwick – once a pilgrims' port, now a golf resort! The final leg of this journey is to Dunbar before cutting across "Border Country" to the west coast where Prestwick, Turnberry, and Troon are featured.

The South East Links

MUIRFIELD THE 2ND, 5TH, 8TH AND 9TH (CLOCKWISE FROM UPPER LEFT); THE NEVER ENDING CHALLENGE OF THE BUNKERING AT MUIRFIELD.

Muirfield has been home to the Honourable Company of Edinburgh Golfers since 1891 when Tom Morris was requested to lay down an 18-hole course for its members situated between the already established Gullane course and Archerfield, a private course and club formed in 1862. They had felt the need to move from the nine hole Musselburgh course they'd played on since 1824, because it was becoming congested. Their founding fathers would have been spotted on Leith Links after the club was formed in 1744, and their forefathers for two centuries before that!

The club's first minute book in March 1744 acknowledged a gift from the City Fathers of Edinburgh; a silver club to be played for annually.

That same year they drew up 13 rules of golf, which were to be adopted by the St. Andrews Society of Golfers (later to become the Royal and Ancient) in 1754. The rules were basic—for example, Rule 11: "If you draw your club, in order to strike and proceed so far into the stroke, as to be bringing down your club; if then your club shall break in any way, it is accounted as a stroke."

At the time that Morris was laying out Muirfield, it was decided that the Open Championship should be extended to four rounds over two days. Most of the competitors would not want to play eight rounds over the nine-hole course at Musselburgh, and so after hosting six Opens, much to the disappointment and anger of the locals, the venue was changed to the new course, under the supervision of the Honourable Company.

Reaction to the course varied. The Scotsman newspaper wrote of it in 1892, "Muirfield provides good golf, sporting shots, tricky but fair greens." Andrew Kirkcaldy, who had been in contention in many a championship and who went on to become the Hon. Professional to the R&A, said of the course that it was "Nothing but a damned water meaddie (meadow). By the time the Open came around again to Muirfield in 1896 the course was lengthened by 800 yards to over 6,000.

By 1922 the club had purchased more ground and hired Harry Colt to redesign Muirfield. Two years later Tom Morris, long since departed from this earth, would hardly have recognised anything of the original course, apart from the old stone dyke (wall) here and there. When Walter Hagen won the Open in 1929, 224 bunkers had to be avoided in the round. When Ernie Els won the last Muirfield Championship there were 148 left.

WILLIE PARK, THE FIRST OPEN CHAMPION IN 1860 WAS RAISED IN MUSSELBURGH AND WENT ON TO WIN FOUR CHAMPIONSHIPS.

Even with the blind drive on the 11th, the course lacks the quirkiness of older links clubs. This is largely due to the fact that the course played today is essentially the same course redesigned in 1925 by H.S. Colt. Rather than an in-line course, Colt has employed a clockwise outer circle front nine with an anti-clockwise inner circle back nine, this provides constantly changing wind angles, not often found on links courses. Justifiably tagged "fair" it must not be misinterpreted as easy and anybody getting greedy will be bitten.

Muirfield #13

Playing slightly uphill and into a narrow bowl of sand dunes, this demanding Par 3 requires pinpoint accuracy, even on the calmest of days. The 5 bunkers that ring both sides of the green are true pot bunkers, small in size, but mighty in their effect. The closely mown surrounding ground gathers all errant shots, leaving difficult recovery shots often from awkward stance from these small reveted bunkers.

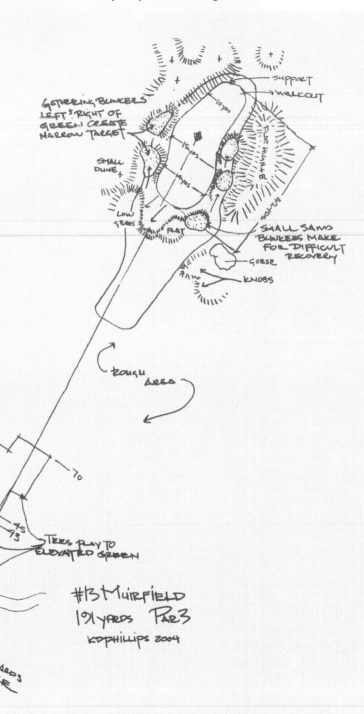

Tom Simpson, another eminent architect, was asked to look over the course in 1935 and many of his recommendations were taken. He felt there were too many bunkers, too many undulations on the greens, and too wide an entrance at certain greens. In praising the course after his win in 1966, Jack Nicklaus said there was an honesty and integrity about Muirfield: "What you see is what you get."

Muirfields Open Champions

The first winner at Muirfield in 1892 went on to win four British Amateur Championships and held the British and American titles in 1911. The 23-year-old Hilton was trailing the leader by seven shots at the halfway stage but came storming through to beat his old adversary and colleague from Royal Liverpool, John Ball, also an amateur, by three shots. Harry Vardon recorded his first of six wins in 1896 (three at Prestwick and two at Sandwich) preventing J.H.Taylor from winning three in a row by beating him in an 18-hole play-off that year. James Braid had two consecutive wins at Muirfield in 1901 and 1906 by hitting the ball with "divine fury," backed up by a masterly short game!

In the 1906 Open, Vardon and Taylor both "strayed" in the final round and Braid took the title nine shots better than in his previous win. The big-pipe smoking, long driving Englishman Ted Ray won in 1912. He and Vardon went out on two extensive tours of America where Ray eventually won the U.S. Open in 1920.

The first American to win in 1929 was Walter Hagen. He did so in convincing fashion, having reached the turn on the final round in 35 with a 10 shot lead! By this time he had won two Opens at Sandwich and one at Hoylake. He brought colour back into the game with his swashbuckling lifestyle and attacking play. Despite being a little-known player outside England, Alf Perry's winning aggregate of 283 in 1935 was not bettered until 1966, when Jack Nicklaus took one shot off it. Perry's score was nine better than Hagen's emphatic win before him.

In 1948 Henry Cotton had been ill but built himself up for this Open and drove as straight as he ever had. A stunning 66 in the second round left everyone trailing in his wake. He was the best British player of two decades with wins at Sandwich in 1934 and Carnoustie in 1938. Over three decades Gary Player won Open Championships, his first being at Muirfield in 1959. When Jack Nicklaus in 1966 won by a shot from

Doug Sanders and Dave Thomas, he said of Muirfield, "I liked it from the first day I played it. It is essentially a fair course, it has more definition than any Links that the Open is played on."

In 1972 Lee Trevino successfully defended his Championship win, despite a familiar "charge" from Nicklaus and a tussle with Tony Jacklin over the last three holes. With rounds of 68, 70, 64, and 67, Tom Watson broke the Muirfield Championship record by seven shots in 1980. Emulating James Braid, Nick Faldo won back-to-back Opens here in 1987 and 1992. Grinding out 18 consecutive pars on the last round in his first victory he took the lead from Paul Azinger on the final hole. In 1992 Faldo had another battle on his hands in the last round, this time with American John Cook who found himself on the seventeenth, two shots clear of the Englishman, having been four behind at the turn! Faldo, playing two holes back in "true grit" fashion, would not let go of his title and again won on the last green.

The Course Today

Ernie Els from South Africa won the last Open at Muirfield in 2002 after a four-way play-off with two Australians and a Frenchman! The course is constantly rated internationally by the golfing media, and is never out of the world's nominated top 10 courses. It is often given the accolade of being the best championship course in Britain. The reputation of the Muirfield course has been enhanced through time. Articles and comments by the leading players over seven decades have declared it fair but demanding. After winning the Open there in 1948, Henry Cotton announced, "The long carries and narrow fairways suited me to perfection. I have decided to retire from competitive golf here and now; I feel I have been fortunate to win and want to end my playing days on a high note."

The layout of the two loops, each of nine holes (one clockwise and one counterclockwise) means that when the wind gets up, there's never any real advantage when negotiating your way around the course hole by hole. Course management, as on the Old Course at St. Andrews, comes into play; the 13 past champions over Muirfield who held the claret jug aloft lay testament to that.

MUIRFIELD THE LATE AUTUMNAL COLOURS CLEARLY DEFINE THE 18TH TEE AND
FAIRWAY WHILE THE SETTING SUN ADDS DRAMA TO THE GREEN AND CLUBHOUSE.

ary Queen of Scots was spotted playing golf upon the links
by Longniddry just one week after the murder of her husband
Lord Darnley in 1567; this was considered "gie (very) suspi-
cious" by the locals, inferring that she may well have had a hand in the
dastardly deed. Two centuries later the 7th Earl of Wemyss bought the
land around this area "to be nearer to gowf". The 11th Earl commissioned
Harry Colt to construct a full eighteen hole course over this historic ground
in 1920. Since then James Braid, Mackenzie Ross and Donald Steele have
left their mark on what has now become an established qualifying course
for the Muirfield Open. Longniddry has played host to the British
Seniors and Commonwealth Youths Tournaments and The Ladies
Home Internationals.

LONGNIDDRY **BELOW**: APPROACH TO THE 1ST GREEN PAR 4, HEAVILY
BUNKERED TO THE RIGHT. **OPPOSITE**: THE ELEVATED 18TH GREEN AND CLUBHOUSE.

Scottish Golf Links

LUFFNESS NEW

Deceptively called "new," the links have been prominent since Luffness Golf Club was formed in 1867. Luffness boasted, at one time, a mighty 12th century castle and a late 13th century Monastery. The course is situated close to the village of Aberlady. In the late eighteen eighties, just two hundred yards from the links, a private tow and a half mile rail link was shared with the Longniddry course. There is such a wealth of courses in the area that it confuses the visiting golfer as to which one he is actually playing. For instance, the old Luffness Club changed its name to Kilspindie Golf Club in 1898 when Ben Sayers added yet another course by Aberlady Bay. Old Tom Morris had set out the original old Luffness course in 1867, at the height of his career, winning his fourth Open Championship that year. He was back again in 1893 to help the landowner, Mr. George Hope, re-shape and preserve the original nine holes and add a further nine on new ground

The report on the opening day's play of the original course in 1867 reads;

"There was a considerable muster of players on the occasion, among whom was the celebrated player Tom Morris of St. Andrews, who acted as umpire for the game. It was found that when the course had been played over the lowest score was Mr. P. Hunter with 108 for seventeen holes (another was added in 1872)."

In the Kilspindie clubhouse today hangs the putter of Old Tom Morris from that winning era. Freddie Tait, a hugely popular British Amateur Champion in the eighteen nineties, learned to play at Luffness and represented the club in many battles. Tragically, he was killed in a real battle in the Boer War in 1900 at aged thirty.

LUFFNESS OPPOSITE: THE FAIRWAY AND CROSS BUNKERING ON THE 1ST FAIRWAY IS BOTH DRAMATIC AND SIMILAR THAT OF THE 17TH AT MUIRFIELD. UPPER RIGHT: THE 4H PLAYING BACK TO THE CLUBHOUSE. RIGHT: THE 18TH IS STEEPLY BANKED AT THE BACK OF THE GREEN TO OFFER SOME PROTECTION TO PASSING CARS.

Scottish Golf Links

GULLANE

In a review of Gullane Links in 1895 it was written that, "It is of the first quality. The soil is of the finest sandy kind (sand, having been blown in from Aberlady Bay), and the grass, cropped short by multitudinous rabbits, affords the best of "lies" and putting greens. The Links are a remarkable testimony to the usefulness of the much-abused rabbit as a greenkeeper. It is to his agency that the turf owes its extraordinary springiness, enabling a man to play golf from morn till dewy eve of the longest summer's day without more than a proper and comfortable sense of fatigue. It is a worthy green for the ladies' championship; it is a worthy green (if this might be said without lapse of gallantry) for a greater championship. The Championship Meeting of the Ladies Golf Union of Great Britain will be held on Gullane Links in 1897." Fifty years later, in a blaze of publicity, American "Babe" Zaharis, a double Olympic gold medal winner, took the national ladies title when it was played there again.

From its original seven-hole course in 1840, Gullane had three courses by 1910: all start and finish in the shadow of the clubhouse. Gullane No. 1, the oldest, and No. 2 (a Willie Park Jr. layout from 1900) have been frequently used in qualifying for the Muirfield Open.

The Dirleton Castle Club was the oldest here, founded in 1854, but golf was played as early as 1650 when the Dirleton weavers took on their local trade rivals of Aberlady on the links. Training and exercising racehorses up on Gullane Hill became a problem that was eventually resolved in 1892 when the gofers won a legal battle by a short head to keep the track solely for golf! "The Hill" is such a feature on the Gullane Links and has a breathtaking view of Dunbar on the east side, to the Kingdom of Fife over the Forth Estuary and the road and rail bridges linking up two kindred golfing spirits.

GULLANE **Opposite:** No. 1, 2 and 3 courses clubhouse and pro shop and town. **Right:** Gullane No. 1 the uphill par four 6th green.

GULLANE **LEFT**: No. 1 COURSE 9TH, SEEMINGLY PERCHED ON THE BANKS OF THE FIRTH OF FORTH. **BELOW**: GULLANE No. 1 COURSE 9TH TEE TO GREEN. **OPPOSITE, LEFT**: GULLANE No. 2 COURSE 11TH TEE TO GREEN PAR 3. **OPPOSITE, RIGHT**: GULLANE No. 3 COURSE LOOKING BACK THROUGH THE 13TH GREEN WITH THE 12TH TO THE LEFT.

When the Earls of Fife sponsored a ferry near Elie to take pilgrims back and forth from North Berwick to witness the great construction of St. Andrews Cathedral in the twelfth century, a bond was struck between the two Royal Burghs. The same pilgrims badges dating back to 1300 were on sale as souvenirs in both North Berwick and St. Andrews for over two centuries! Up to 10,000 people a year were transported across the Forth to visit the saints' relics that were reputedly enshrined in the cathedral. The term "pilgrim" was used loosely; "holidaymaker" would have sounded cheap! With precious little leisure time allotted to the average workingman and his family, a "pilgrimage" was a fine justification for taking a break from the drudgery and monotony of daily life.

The North Berwick Golf Club was founded in 1832, followed by the Tantallon Golf Club in 1853 and with the help of the Bass Rock Club, contributed to the upkeep of the courses. Part of the East Course is the oldest, the West Course the most celebrated, and used in qualifying for the Muirfield Open.

NORTH BERWICK **OPPOSITE**: AN AERIAL VIEW OF, IN THE FOREGROUND, THE 1ST AND 17TH GREENS WITH THE18TH GREEN, CLUBHOUSE AND TOWN BEYOND. **UPPER RIGHT**: THIS MEDAL (TOP) DATED 1850, WAS PRESENTED TO NORTH BERWICK BY THE EARL OF EGLINTON, WHO AT THAT TIME HAD JUST EMPLOYED OLD TOM MORRIS TO MOVE FROM ST. ANDREWS TO LAY OUT THE COURSE AT PRESTWICK AND BECOME ITS "KEEPER OF THE GREENS". **RIGHT**: DATED 1868, THIS IS BELIEVED TO BE THE OLDEST JUNIOR GOLF MEDAL IN EXISTENCE.

Scottish Golf Links

Challenge Matches

Great challenge matches were played over St. Andrews, Musselburgh, and North Berwick in the 1850s and '60s. Instead of the arduous, slow journey of the past, attempting to get from one venue to the next, trains had linked up this mini golfing circuit for one and all.

Two-ball foursomes being the main form of match play saw the Park brothers of Musselburgh square up to the Dunn twins of North Berwick, or Allan Robertson and Tom Morris representing St. Andrews. Over 36 holes on a Saturday, huge crowds turned up for those advertised, much-awaited games and had to be policed because rivalries between the teams supporters became heated and hostile as the day wore on!

Normally a "challenge" match would be over 12 rounds in six days (24 rounds of the nine-hole North Berwick and Musselburgh courses). Tom Morris and Willie Park played 36 rounds in a confrontation split equally within the three venues over a three-week period, with just the two Sundays off to get from one course to the next!

One of the most publicised matches at North Berwick was between Tom Morris Sr. and Jr. against the Park brothers on the sixth of September in 1875. Young Tom was in his prime, having already won four Opens, at age 24. He received a telegram that his wife was struggling in childbirth with his first son and he had to make his way "posthaste" back to St. Andrews.

A Mr. Lewis, who had sponsored the match, put his schooner and full crew at the Morris's disposal to take them across the Firth of Forth and into St. Andrews Bay to be picked up in a rowing boat. As they set sail, unbeknownst to them another telegram arrived saying that both his wife and child had died. Sixteen weeks later Young Tom himself passed away on Christmas morning. Reflecting on his life in 1906, old Tom said mournfully, "people say young Tommy died of a broken heart, but if that was so…I wouldna be here either!"

NORTH BERWICK **OPPOSITE**: WAVES GENTLY LAPPING ON THE BEACH BUT THE CHOICE ON THE 2ND TEE IS HOW MUCH OF THE DO YOU WANT TO TRY TO CUT OFF ON THE WAY TO THE SAFETY OF THE FAIRWAY? **ABOVE**: THE 6TH "QUARRY" IS A SHORT PAR 3 WITH A BUNKER 10 FEET BELOW THE GREEN.

NORTH BERWICK | *An Architectural View by Kyle Phillips*

North Berwick has the most creative collection of greens architecture I have ever seen. The most famous being the Redan. The scale of the course is similar to that of Prestwick with one of the most welcoming atmospheres to visitors around the member's clubhouse. The course is an extension of the town resulting in a magical atmosphere comparable only to that of the Old Course at St. Andrews.

North Berwick #13

This, the simplest green on the course, is nestled at the base of a large dune, with a diagonal stone wall extending from behind the green into the landing area. It is unusual that we find one simple feature dominating the entire strategy of a hole. Diagonal hazards are used commonly in golf course design, but often at angles closer to 30 and 45 degrees off of the line of play. This feature works off an angle closer to 15 degrees. This long hazard forces long drives down the right side of the fairway into a constantly narrowing area that naturally feeds into the bunkers, leaving the shorter approach with a more difficult angle into the green. The preferred line to open up the approach to the green is from the left portion of fairway, but this area has been further defended with the addition of a new bunker in 2004.

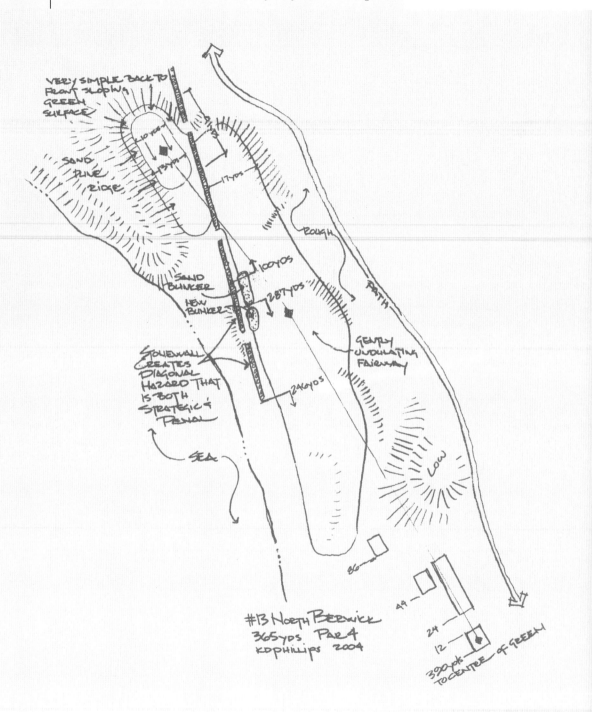

This aerial view shows the 13th fairway and green, divided by the wall, at the centre of the picture. To the right is the short par 3 "Quarry" 6th hole and in the far distance the renowned "Redan" 15th.

THE 13TH GREEN, SIMPLY PROTECTED BY THE USE OF
THIS OLD WALL, IS AFFECTIONATELY KNOWN AS "THE PIT".

NORTH BERWICK THE 15TH REDAN IS NAMED AFTER THE
REDOUBT OF THE SAME NAME FROM THE SIEGE OF SEBASTOPOL
(1854, 1855), IN THE CRIMEA WAR. THIS IS THEREFORE THE
ORIGINAL REDAN HOLE. THE MILITARY DESCRIPTION OF A REDAN
DESCRIBES IT "A SMALL FORTRESS, WITH TWO SALIENT WALLS
AND A GORGE SET AT AN ANGLE TO THE ENEMY."

NORTH BERWICK ALTHOUGH ALL OF THE REAL
DANGER IS OUT OF VIEW THIS IS A GREAT VISUAL
HOLE. THE GREEN IS HIDDEN FROM THE TEE WITH
THE TWO FACING BUNKERS (PICTURED ON THE OPPO-
SITE PAGE) NOT REALLY COMING INTO PLAY. BEHIND
THEM IS A DEEP GULLY RISING BACK UP TO A GREEN
WITH A PRONOUNCED RIGHT TO LEFT AND SLIGHT
FRONT TO BACK INCLINE. THE GREENSIDE BUNKERS
ARE A CONSIDERABLE HAZARD WITH THE SINGLE ONE
TO THE LEFT SIDE THE MOST CHALLENGING AND FRE-
QUENTLY VISITED.

That year (1906) saw new life and activity on the East Course as it added another nine holes. North Berwick had become known as "The Biarritz of the North" and aristocrats and socialites met up during the summer months. At the turn of the twentieth century dukes, lords and ladies, princes and princesses, right honourables, and even the king himself (Edward VII) had visited the Royal Burgh. For example: extract from a local paper in 1903: "On the links this week at one moment there were, in the course of play, The Prime Minister, the Speaker of the House of Commons, four Members of Parliament; two Bishops of the Church of England, three eminent professors, a field marshal, two generals, and a Tibetan Explorer." A. J. Balfour, the prime minister, was a regular summer visitor to the resort and was often photographed playing on the links. The prestigious Marine Hotel had been built looking out over the West Course to accommodate this influx of gentry in the 1890s, much in the same way as St. Andrews had kept up with demand by building the Rusacks Marine Hotel and the Grand Hotel around the last hole of the Old Course. It was certainly a boom time in both towns and wee Ben Sayers, professional, clubmaker and teacher in North Berwick benefited from his popularity by securing his business' future. Although he had never won an Open, Sayers had been in contention in just about every championship over a 20-year period from 1883. Frequently paired with Willie Auchterlonie from St. Andrews, they were rarely beaten in match play anywhere in the country.

NORTH BERWICK LEFT: THE USE OF NATURAL TERRAIN CONTINUES ON THE 16TH GREEN. THE TWO ELEVATED PUTTING SURFACES ARE SEPARATED BY ANOTHER GULLY. OPPOSITE: THE 18TH TEE TO GREEN IS VERY SIMILAR TO ST. ANDREWS. A ROLLING FAIRWAY, OUT-OF-BOUNDS RIGHT, LEADS TO A RAISED GREEN WITH PROTECTIVE VALLEY TO THE FRONT.

Caddies

In an editorial in the Haddingtonshire Courier in 1905, the caddies of North Berwick were described as being "noted for their superfluous clothing, their readiness at advice and sarcasm and their infinitive capacity for fiery liquors." Sadly, the editor goes on to suggest that their days are numbered and that not before time a new breed of caddie was evolving. "They may be less picturesque and less loquacious than those of the older sort but they are cleaner, soberer and more respectful. There was far too much misery and pauperism connected with the lives of the old-fashioned caddie to allow of any feeling but one of thankfulness at the fact that the profession is becoming more respectable."

When the West Course was extended to 18 holes in 1877 it was frequently described as short and "somewhat flukey," with a peculiar character. Despite its lack of yardage at that time, some greens were extremely difficult to hit on plateaus surrounded by bunkers, banks, and walls. Now 6,420 yards, with a standard scratch of 71, it has become a course of great distinction.

NORTH BERWICK THE GLEN **Opposite**: The 1st green, sitting high above the tee and clubhouse, requires a blind approach shot. **Above**: The majority of the course plays above the Firth of Forth with views out to The Bass Rock.

DUNBAR FROM THE ELEVATED 3RD TEE LOOKING
DOWN ON THE HEAVILY BUNKERED GREEN AND OUT TO
THE NORTH SEA.

DUNBAR

Around the coastal corner from North Berwick heading south is Dunbar our first or last stop in Scotland (depending on whether you're coming or going). Evidence of bronze age burials have been found in close proximity to the links. The Picts had a large fortress in this area, and later in the Middle Ages, Dunbar had one of the most important for keeping the invading English out!

The Dunbar Golf Club called for Tom Morris, at that time, keeper of the green at Prestwick (1856), to lay out a 15 hole course for them. There had been a club, the Dunbar Golfing Society founded in 1794, but it hadn't lasted long because by all accounts, "dining out" after matches had become too expensive and so the club was disbanded! Golf had been played around this coastline for centuries; evident when the local minister disgraced himself by being caught on the links on the Sabbath in 1640. He was publicly reprimanded and humiliated by the Burgh Council in full view of his parishioners!

Having aquired more ground in 1880 to add three holes to make up the standard 18 holes which had become the norm by then, Dunbar Links has changed little in its structure since. As well as being used as a qualifying course for the Muirfield Open, it has played host to all the major Scottish Amateur Championships.

DUNBAR THE 1ST — A LONG SLIGHTLY UPHILL PAR 4.

DUNBAR THE APPROACH TO THE 14TH GREEN OFFERS A WONDERFUL PERSPECTIVE ACROSS THE BAY TO THE TOWN OF DUNBAR.

Portpatrick golf course with magnificent views over the Irish Sea.

From Dunbar and east to west, travel across the Scottish Border Country with its rolling hills and fertile valleys, through the textile and rugby towns of Galashiels and Melrose to Dumfries 15 miles down the Solway Firth. From there, north to the Ayrshire coast and Burns Country. Robert Burns, an eighteenth-century poet, now known as the national bard of Scotland, wrote and farmed around Ayr during his short and troubled life.

THIS LAST PART OF MY JOURNEY COVERS AN EXTENSIVE AREA FROM THE FAR SOUTH WEST COAST OF SCOTLAND, PAST THE COURSES OF POWFOOT, PORTPATRICK AND STRANRAER AND THEN FURTHER NORTH AROUND GLASGOW AND OUT TO THE TIP OF THE MULL OF KINTYRE. THE FOUR MAJOR COURSES OF TURNBERRY, PRESTWICK, ROYAL TROON AND MACHRIHANISH ARE SUCH AESTHETICALLY STUNNING AND HISTORICALLY IMPORTANT COURSES THAT I HAVE DEVOTED TWO THIRDS OF THE CHAPTER TO THEM BUT STILL ALLOWED TIME FOR A FEW DIVERSIONS AND A GLIMPSE OF THE STUNNING COUNTRYSIDE.

Islay

EDINBURGH ■

GLASGOW ■

Machrie

Arran

Western Gailes & Glasgow Gailes
Dundonald
Royal Troon
Prestwick

Machrihanish

Turnberry

Portpatrick

Southerness

Irish Sea

Across to the West Coast

SOUTHERNESS

Along the Scottish bank of the Solway Firth (the south side is the English Cumbrian coast) to Southerness Point sits a classic links course. With a 360° view, following the Galloway Hills, Criffel being the most dominant, they turn you toward the sea, and on a clear day the Isle of Man is visible out in the Irish Sea. Across the Firth, which changes its personality by the turn of a tide, lie the mountains of the Lake District. Add to this the constant sound of seabirds, the hovering of a rare red kite, or the gaggle of hundreds of geese during the winter months as you tramp along the edge of heather-lined fairways. The tail end of the Gulf Stream enables golf to be played all year round and enables some unexpectedly rare plants to grow around the area. The Southerness links is full of surprises. It was laid out by Paul Mackenzie Ross in 1949, which is a surprise in itself as the course gives the impression of being established at least 70 years before that. About that time Ross, who had worked with Tom Simpson in the 20s and 30s, restructured the courses at Dumfries and Turnberry.

SOUTHERNESS THE HEATHER IN FULL BLOOM PROVIDES A TRADITIONAL LOOK TOWARDS THE CLUBHOUSE. LEFT: THE SUBTLETY OF THE SMALL DIP THAT PROTECTS THE FRONT OF THE 7TH GREEN COMBINES WITH CLASSICAL BUNKERING TO MAKE THIS A CHALLENGING COURSE. OPPOSITE: THE 12TH GREEN, PERCHED ON THE EDGE OF THE SOLWAY FIRTH, IS A TOUGH PAR 4 VERY EXPOSED TO THE FULL FORCE OF THE WIND.

The Lighthouse and The Ailsa Craig are the two easily recognisable features in this aerial view. In the foreground the 11th hole, a par 3 with its tee seemingly perched on the edge of the water and just behind it the 10th green, protected by an island bunker, with the tee up on the hill. The challenging uphill 12th hole is to the left of the picture.

TURNBERRY

I n the same year as winning the Open at Musselburgh in 1883, Willie Fernie from St. Andrews, at that time professional at Troon, supervised the construction of a private 13-hole course for the Marquis of Ailsa on his land at Turnberry. Now a championship links, it is named after the Marquis—and what looks like an enormous chunk of granite floating on the Firth of Clyde-the Ailsa Craig, prominent from the course.

The Glasgow and South Western Railway Company persuaded the Marquis to lease them a prime piece of his estate and, after two years constructing the Turnberry Hotel, opened it to the public in 1906. The company had added another 13-hole course, the Arran, and ran a "golfers express" from Glasgow and a direct sleeper service from London to encourage use of their impressive new golf resort.

Problems arose with the advent of the Great War, when the Royal Flying Corps arrested the courses as a much-needed training facility! After repairing the damage, along came the second war and the links were flattened to make way for three runways for the Royal Air Force. With wartime nationalisation of the railways the whole Turnberry complex was under threat till Frank Hole, its manager, successfully appealed to the British Government for compensation to rebuild their courses. Paul MacKenzie Ross, who had just completed the much talked about Southerness Links, worked with Hole in 1951 to create what was to become an outstanding championship course. A hole like the ninth, "Bruces Castle," where from this frightening tee, exposed to the elements, in the shadow of a lighthouse, you attempt to drive across the Atlantic Ocean to reach the fairway! Since the successful rebirth of Turnberry it has hosted PGA Match Plays, the Walker Cup, the British Amateur, and three Opens. Added to the wonderful facilities of the grand old hotel that dominates the landscape is the Colin Montgomerie Links Golf Academy.

TURNBERRY **ABOVE:** THE TEE TO GREEN VIEW OF THE UPHILL 200 YARD 6TH. **RIGHT:** LOOKING BACK THROUGH THE 6TH GREEN AND BUNKERS TOWARDS THE HOTEL AND CLUBHOUSE.

Turnberry Opens

"The Duel in the Sun" was how the last day's play in the Open of 1977 is remembered, with Tom Watson and Jack Nicklaus battling it out, 10 shots clear of the rest of the field. Watson finished with two rounds of 65 to big Jack's 65, 66. This dramatic head-to-head match was watched on television all around the world, and it secured and enhanced the reputation of Turnberry as a championship venue. When the Open returned in 1986, Greg Norman proved to be a popular winner. Driving long and as straight as an arrow he coasted to victory, having set a new course record of 63 in the second round despite three-putting the last green. Nick Price, originally from Zimbabwe, but well established on the European and American tours, lifted the claret jug in 1994 with a strong finish, eagling the 17th.

TURNBERRY IT IS LATE AUTUMN AND THIS VIEW THROUGH THE 10TH GREEN TO THE LIGHTHOUSE AND DISTANT AILSA CRAIG CAPTURES THE CLASSIC AND WELL RECOGNISED FEATURES OF TURNBERRY GOLF COURSE.

TURNBERRY THE 12TH IS A RELATIVELY SHORT BUT TESTING PAR 4.

THE TEE TO GREEN VIEW OF THE 15TH WITH THE HOTEL IN THE DISTANCE.
THE LOW MORNING SUN CASTS A CLEAR SHADOW WHICH HELPS TO EMPHASISE
THE DANGER OF COMING UP SHORT OR DRIFTING RIGHT ON THIS PAR 3.

The first time I played the Ailsa, the conditions couldn't have been much worse. Even though I was barely able to stand up against the wind and horizontal rain, the fairness of the course came through. Since then I have been able to confirm my feelings about the course under less strenuous conditions. The architecture is not as intricate as some of the other famous links, as the course is laid out on a grand scale with a strategy more similar to modern courses. It is one of my favourite links courses, partially because of the subtleties of the design. I find many of the holes appear to be easier than they are, luring me to be braver at times than I should, but always giving each shot its just reward.

Turnberry Ailsa #16

The 16th is indicative of the subtleness of the course. A hole that I find always plays much more difficult than it appears. From the tee, the bunker on the left provides definition to the fairway as a good drive will go well past this bunker and just disappear over the horizon, giving little clues as to the difficulty that lies ahead on the approach shot. A drive that cheats the right side of the fairway will set up a favourable approach by reducing the diagonal of the burn and playing more directly into the green contours. Faced with a slightly down hill lie, with the tightly mown slope gathering all weak shots into the burn, this approach shot is one of the best and most memorable in links golf.

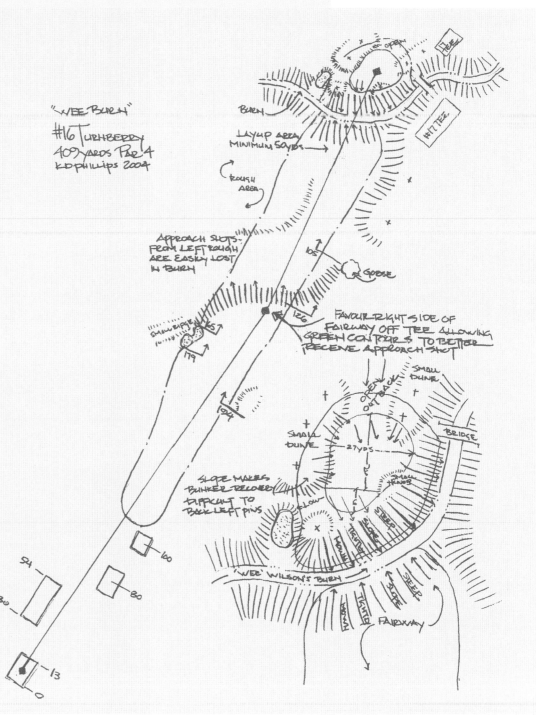

LEFT: THIS AERIAL VIEW SHOW THE BURN WRAPPING AROUND THE FRONT AND RIGHT SIDE OF THE 16TH GREEN. THE 6TH GREEN CAN BE SEEN IN THE UPPER LEFT CORNER.
BELOW: THE BURN, SHADOWED, PROTECTS THE FRONT OF THE 16TH GREEN.

THE BEAUTY OF THE 17TH GREEN AT DAWN.

PRESTWICK ST. NICHOLAS

Prestwick St. Nicholas (Nicholas being the patron saint of Prestwick) was formed just five months after the main club in 1851. It was originally the Prestwick Mechanics Golf Club, being the first of the "artisan" clubs, but this was considered inappropriate as they had attracted professional and businessmen to the club within five years of becoming established. Despite this, St. Nicholas only paid Prestwick Golf Club £5 per annum for playing rights on the course. In 1877 Charlie Hunter, who had represented the St. Nicholas club in the first Open, helped them build their own course—an amicable agreement between the two clubs as the Prestwick club, of which Hunter had become "keeper" and professional, helped pay for its construction.

PRESTWICK ST. NICHOLAS THE 16TH IS, WITH THE FAIRWAY HIDDEN FROM VIEW, A SEMI-BLIND DRIVING HOLE. ACCURACY AND DISTANCE ARE AN ISSUE AS ANYTHING TOO LONG OR SLIGHTLY WAYWARD RISKS THE GORSE AND ROUGH ENCROACH ON THIS NARROWING AND UNDULATING LANDING AREA. ALSO PICTURED, THE 17TH PAR THREE WITH THE 18TH PLAYING BACK UP TO THE CLUBHOUSE.

THE DRAMATIC SLOPE OF THE 15TH
GREEN IS LOST AMONGST THE SUNLIT BEAUTY OF
SCOTTISH COLOURS IN THE LATE SUMMER.

Q uotation from the *Golfing Annual* of 1887: "It is legend that to settle a deadly feud a match took place on 'ye links at Ayr' several hundred years ago, between a monk of Crossaguel and a Lord of Culzean." So golf was played on the west coast in a similar fashion to the east coast in the sixteenth century but did not have a recognised or "official" course until Prestwick in 1851. Long before, King Robert the Bruce had given his loyal and battle-scared archers from around Ayr the linksland at Prestwick, "the common land" to use for recreation.

It's a familiar story by now on this Scottish coastal trail that with the railway, in this case the Glasgow and Southwest, it linked up the thriving city of Glasgow to Ayr in 1849. It was a dramatic year in the evolution of the game as suddenly courses up both coastlines (and across to them) would be accessible and the new gutta ball affordable. The Earl of Eglinton, who owned substantial grounds and a castle, waved down the first trains from Glasgow that steamed through his estate and demanded free rides down to Ayr and back—as was his right! He had access to a patch of rough linksland about three miles to the north of Ayr and decided now that he had "transport," it would be an idea to invite Tom Morris across to lay out a proper course. The Earl's great friend and foursomes partner, James Ogilvie Fairlie (captain of the Royal and Ancient in St. Andrews at that time), persuaded Morris to move to Prestwick with his family to become "keeper of the green"—a position old Tom would hold for 13 years before returning to St. Andrews and maintaining the Old Course for 38 years.

Morris was to lay out 12 holes in a cramped and restricted area but took full advantage of the contours and ambience of the site that included stunning views across the sea to the Isle of Arran. Shortly before he started work, 50 members, newly enrolled by Fairlie, met for the first time on the second of July, 1851 in the Red Lion Inn, just a drive and a cleek from the proposed course. The early days of the Prestwick club were "troubled," as by scanning the minutes of the secretaries' reports in the 1850s there seemed to be a great reluctance by the membership to pay their annual subscription of a pound!

Tom Morris worked tirelessly to improve the course. He found that sand was a great protector of links turf against biting winds and hard frost. He discovered this by accident after spilling a barrowload of it at the side of a green he was having trouble establishing. Having spread the sand

PRESTWICK **ABOVE**: THE PLAQUE COMMEMORATING THE ORIGINAL POSITION OF THE 1ST TEE. **BELOW**: THE CHALLENGE OF THE 1ST HOLE WITH THE OUT-OF-BOUNDS WALL TO THE RIGHT.

PRESTWICK Cardinals Bunker, on the 3rd hole, may
not come into play on this dogleg right par 5 but the
undulating of fairways leading to a bunker free green
may pose some problems.

around instead of shovelling it back into his barrow, he found that over the winter the grass around this area seemed to revive itself. From that moment on top-dressing became a standard greenkeeping practice and "sand...more sand!" was to be the Morris battle cry or instruction on every links course he was involved with from then on!

Local man Charlie Hunter was to become "the grand old man of Prestwick." He had played in the first Open, took over from Morris, and was to remain keeper of the green till 1921, becoming one of the most recognisable characters on the west coast of Scotland. It is astonishing how few professionals Prestwick had over a period of 150 years. After Hunter's 54 years, James McDowell had a "brief" stay (six years) and was replaced by Robert McInnes, who after 35 years handed it over to Frank Rennie. With over 40 years' service to the club, Rennie was asked, if possible, to give an unbiased opinion of the course. Here is what he said, "I have been the professional at Prestwick for over 40 years. I have played in events in many parts of the world; I know of no other course that requires more caution. At 6,500 yards it is not unduly long for a championship course, but any advantage that may exist on that score is more than compensated by the hidden disasters that await the unsuspecting player."

"Hidden disasters" such as the Cardinals Bunker and its facing of railway sleepers on the third, is one of the signature holes on the course. This was one of the original holes in the 12-hole course in 1851. Another is the 17th, "Alps," which was the second hole in the first Open. A blind second shot is all carry over the massive "Sahara Bunker" protecting a green short in depth.

The clubhouse, built in 1868, extended from time to time, houses records and memorabilia recently re-catalogued and converted to disk. This includes gems such as the sketches of The Challenge Belt (the original Open trophy) and the first printed scorecards, including Young Tom Morris's winning cards. Hung around the club's wood panelled walls are portraits of all the key figures who left their mark, not only in Prestwick but in the world of golf. The first large oil painting that awaits you in the foyer is the formidable looking secretary from 1868 to 1902, Harry Hart. He was immediately made captain of the club when he retired!

PRESTWICK THE THIRD FAIRWAY MAY BE BUNKER FREE BUT STILL POSSESSES A CONSIDERABLE CHALLENGE.

Through half closed eyes, and ignoring Prestwick Airport in the distance, you can imagine this famous Links as it was when hosting the first Open Championship in 1860. Only the texture of the green and a more hospitable fairway bring you back to earth or to more modern times. There is an aura, a great sense of tradition surrounding this compact linksland that is Prestwick Golf Course. Distant sounds of a "clunk" or "click" as an early hand hammered gutta being struck by a leather faced playclub (driver) might echo round the first tee and clubhouse...or was it the rattle of a cleek, rutting iron, baffie and putter that would conjure up the past—clubs tucked under arm, ready for play?

PRESTWICK | *An Architectural View by Kyle Phillips*

Around at Prestwick is a trip back in golfing time. This is golf the way was before the advent of 'par' and before the idea 'fair' was narrowly defined by those card and pencil players who were never able accept responsibility for their own lack of skill. By the definition of many of today's "experts", it is an "unfair" course. Blind shots to greens protected by cavernous bunkers (the 14 & 16th greens are the most heavily sloped I have ever seen) with fairways that buck and heave are exactly what makes it one of the world's finest courses, one both young and old enjoy playing. For every aspiring architect, Prestwick is a museum of architecture that deserves study and is guaranteed to excite one's creative juices.

Prestwick #5

Playing over an imposing steep dune face (affectionately called the Himalayas), the 5th is one of the most famous blind par 3's in golf. It will most certainly retain its fame, as any course designed today with such a blind hole would quickly succumb to the modern idea of what is 'fair' in golf course architecture and be redesigned to make the green visible from the tee. When the conditions are firm and the rough deep, a shot played over the Himalayas and landing just short and right of the green has a reasonable chance to avoid the bunkers and find the putting surface.

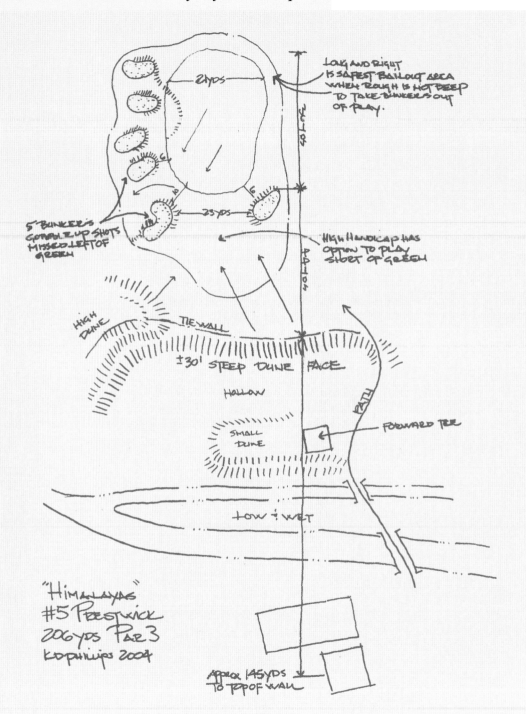

THE MOUNTAINS OF ARRAN, DUSTED WITH SNOW,
PROVIDE A DRAMATIC BACKDROP TO THE CHALLENGING UPHILL 10TH HOLE.

With the untimely death of Allan Robertson in 1859, aged forty-two, it was decided by the Prestwick club to set up a challenge the following year to see who would take over his mantle as the champion golfer of his day. Letters were sent to Blackheath, Perth, Bruntsfield, Musselburgh and St. Andrews inviting a "respectable caddie" to represent each of their clubs on the 12th of October 1860 to compete against each other in stroke play. That may sound patronising, and indeed it was! The early years of The Open were played as a form of entertainment for the members after their Autumn Meeting.

The Earl of Eglington presented an impressive belt of soft red Moroccan leather with a detailed golfing scene engraved on its silver buckle. It was the type of trophy he might have competed for jousting or in archery some thirty years earlier. The Earl had become the first official sponsor of a professional golf tournament when the eight competitors lined up in heavy green checked foresters jackets—normally worn by workers on his estate. The length of the course at that time was 3,799 yards, the longest hole being the 1st at 578 yards, formidable, as the average drive of a crack professional was between one hundred and eighty and two hundred yards (all carry with very little run on the ball.) When Tom Morris Jr. was going for his third Open Championship in a row in 1870 he eagled the first in the opening round, which was awesome with the equipment he used at that time! The shortest hole, the 11th, was recorded as ninety-seven yards. Many of the holes were blind shots from the tee to the green as sand hills or dunes had to be "lofted" over. As usual it was imperative to keep the ball in play as there were no preferred lies dictated by one of the 13 basic rules laid down in 1744.

PRESTWICK **OPPOSITE**: THE VIEW FROM THE 16TH TEE, ACROSS THIS RUGGED LINKS-LAND, SEEMS TO ENCOURAGE AN UNACHIEVABLE ATTACKING LINE TO THE GREEN, SEEN ON THE EXTREME RIGHT OF THE PICTURE. **BELOW**: THE SAFER ROUTE IS TOWARDS WILLIE CAMPBELL'S GRAVE, IN THE CENTRE OF THE FAIRWAY, WHICH THEN ALLOWS A STRAIGHTFORWARD APPROACH TO THE GREEN AND, HOPEFULLY, AVOIDS THE DANGERS OF CARDINALS BUNKER TO THE RIGHT.

PRESTWICK THE APPROACH TO THE 17TH GREEN IS TOTALLY BLIND. IT IS ONLY FROM THE TOP OF THE ALPS THAT THE ENORMOUS SAHARA BUNKER COMES ONTO VIEW AND THE SUCCESS OR FAILURE OF YOUR EFFORTS BECOMES APPARENT.

The Prestwick Open Champions

Willie Park emerged victorious in the first Open and was declared "The Champion Golfer of the Year" with three rounds of 55, 59, and 60. Reported as "going for every shot," he beat Tom Morris by two shots and Andrew Strath of St. Andrews by six. Willie Steele from Bruntsfield, who finished 16 over sixes must have been there just to make up the numbers and was never heard of again!

In the first eight Opens, all played at Prestwick, Tom Morris won four to Willie Parks's three, with only Andrew Strath interrupting their monopoly in 1865. One of the many claims to fame of Morris (though not from him, for he was a modest man) was that he left the field trailing by 13 shots in the 1862 Open. This is still the record-winning margin today, and the fact that there were only four professionals playing that day was a minor detail from his point of view! Morris is still the oldest winner of the Open, aged 46 in 1867, then along came his son Tommy the following year to become the youngest ever winner at 17 years old. Still a teenager in 1870, he had won three Opens in a row and the challenge belt was his to keep. Because of this, there was no championship the following year, not just because there was no trophy to play for; sadly, James Ogilvie Fairlie, the sole administrator of the Open, died that year.

Prestwick invited Musselburgh and St. Andrews to host and share the running of the tournament and to club together for a new trophy. The Claret Jug was introduced in 1872 and is still played for today. Young Tom won again making it four in a row at Prestwick and seemed invincible. The Open was rotated between the three courses until Musselburgh was kicked into touch by Muirfield in 1892 and Sandwich and Hoylake in England were included shortly after.

In 1875, when it returned to Prestwick, Willie Park won his fourth Open there—15 years after his first. He was followed by two champions, who both won consecutive Opens on the three venues, Jamie Anderson in 1778 representing St. Andrews, and Bob Ferguson from Musselburgh in 1881. Jack Simpson, based in Carnoustie, was a surprise winner in 1884, followed by Willie Parks's son three years later. Parks Jr. is often mentioned as a course architect on this journey around the Scottish Links. John Ball, the first Englishman to claim the title and usurp the Scots in 1890, was also the first Amateur to win. By 1893 the Open was played over four rounds in two days and 21-year old Willie Auchterlonie from St. Andrews won using

PRESTWICK THE 18TH IS A SHORT PAR 4 AND,
FOR THE BIGGER HITTERS, MAY BE DRIVEABLE BUT ANY
ERRANT SHOTS WILL BE PUNISHED.

just five clubs (which he had made himself). He would be the last home-based Scot to win for 95 years, an unbelievable fact if put to the Scots professionals of that time…but things were changing fast—more people were playing, more clubs were formed, and even more courses were constructed.

With the emergence of the Triumvirate, Harry Vardon was the most successful, winning three out of the four Opens hosted by Prestwick from 1898 to 1914. In the first of these wins he beat Park Jr. by a shot—"the cut" had been introduced by then, dropping all players 20 shots behind the leader after two rounds! Vardon won more convincingly in 1903 by six shots, but James Braid stopped his run emphatically, winning by eight shots in 1908. The last Open before the first World War went to Vardon, with J. H. Taylor as runner-up. Francis Ouimet had come across from the States but finished well down the field.

That Last Ill-fated Championship

With the outbreak of the war and two more new venues coming onto the Open circuit, Prestwick waited 11 years before their ill-fated 1925 championship. MacDonald Smith, a native of Carnoustie—by then an American citizen—made the long journey across the sea to find himself leading by six shots with the final round to come. J. H. Taylor recalled that an estimated 15,000 spectators stopped him from winning! "It was unfortunate for Mac that he was timed to start just when the Glasgow trains were disgorging their human cargo on to the inadequate Prestwick platform, the result being that thousands omitted the formality of tendering their tickets and jumped the intervening wall. Bustled and jostled and hemmed in by the whooping multitude, he was given little room to swing and not once was he allowed the opportunity of seeing the result of his longer shots." It was said that Smith walked off the last green tired and embittered, having taken an 82 and so lost to Jim Barnes, an Englishman who had also become an American citizen! The great golf writer Bernard Darwin said at the time, "I gravely doubt whether a championship should be played here again. GOLF CAN BE ALTOGETHER TOO POPULAR."…and so it was to be—despite being the original home of the Open, the club did not ask to be its host again.

The Amateur

The British Amateur Championship had as much status as the Open title until the turn of the century and Prestwick figured prominently with their Open Champion of 1890, John Ball winning when they hosted their National Amateur Championship two years before. Ball figured in an epic final against F. G. Tait in 1899—winning at the thirty-seventh hole. By 1987, ten British Amateurs had been played at Prestwick, which included two popular American winners—Lawson Little in 1934 and Harvey Ward in 1952.

This aerial view of Royal Troon Golf Course shows, in the foreground, The Postage Stamp 8th tee and green.

Aquotation from Horace Hutchison in The British Golf Links Book of 1896: "For the jaded professional man after his winter's work at the Bar or in chambers, or the busy merchant after his labours in the countinghouse, there is no better restorative than a rest at Troon on its breezy links."

The Troon Golf Club was founded with just 20 members in 1878. Twenty years later they had 700 members, mostly staying around Glasgow, Kilmarnock, Irvine, and Ayr. Their patron, His Grace the Duke of Portland, owned the links as part of the Fullerton Estate and leased them to the club for a nominal rent. By 1888 a clubhouse had been built and Willie Fernie, then their professional, had converted what had originally been a 9 then 12-hole course into the standard 18. With an overall length of 5,656 yards, this premier course today, measures over 7,000 yards. It boasts the longest hole in Open Championship golf, named "Turnberry," at 577 yards; and the shortest, "The Postage Stamp," at 128 yards.

Troon is the only "Royal" on the west coast, having been so honoured during its 100th anniversary in 1978 by Her Majesty Queen Elizabeth II.

The Troon Opens

"The American Invasion" and the dominance in particular of Walter Hagen and Bobby Jones at the Opens in the 1920s was briefly interrupted in 1923 at Troon. Englishman Arthur Havers held off Hagen, the defending champion, by a shot. Hagen, who was to win four times up to 1929 was irritated that professionals were not allowed in the Troon clubhouse. Invited in just for the presentation of the claret jug, he declined and chose to invite to the local pub anyone who fancied a pint! Only two Americans came over for the next Open at Troon in 1950, and they were both amateurs. Bobby Locke from South Africa, winning by two shots, successfully defended the title he had won at Sandwich. With the American Tour established, the Open failed to attract the leading players until Arnold Palmer breathed life back into it when he just failed to win at St. Andrews in the Centenary Open. That was not to say that Locke was not a worthy winner, for he had been out in the States two years before becoming champion and won six tournaments there.

By the time Palmer strode onto the first tee at Troon in 1962 the crowds were back and television had made it international viewing.

THE OPEN CHAMPIONSHIP IN FULL SWING BUT THE ROAR OF THE OUT-BOUND FEDEX AIRCRAFT BRINGS A TEMPORARY HALT TO PLAY. THE MAIL MUST GET THROUGH.

ROYAL TROON

The memorable holes at Royal Troon begin at the par five 6th hole. Typical of many links courses, it plays behind the primary dune and has very little visual contact with the sea. The fairways are generally narrow when compared to many links courses, thus minimizing the number of holes where there are multiple lines of play.

Troon #8

This is my favourite short hole in all of golf. A small green ringed by a variety of difficult recoveries, this hole must be experienced first hand to appreciate just how daunting it really is, and all the more so, with a stiff Scottish breeze coming off the sea and into your face. I like in particular the low detached bunker on the right. This is a good example of the importance and impact of mowing heights in design. Because the long slope leading down to the bunker is tightly mown, rather than maintained with long rough, it gathers up everything that comes near it, leaving a frightening recovery shot.

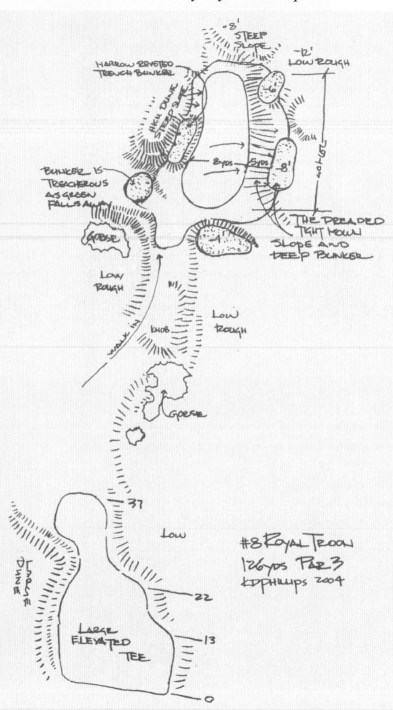

THE TEE TO GREEN VIEW OF THE POSTAGE STAMP
AND TWO OF THE GREENSIDE BUNKERS.

Having won at Birkdale the year before, Palmer dominated the Troon championship, leaving all in his wake. His St. Andrews caddie of 35 years, "Tip" Anderson, said that it was the best he had ever seen "Mr. Palmer" play. With rounds of 71, 69, 67, and 69 on hard fairways, thick rough, and fast greens, only Kel Nagle got within six shots of him with third-placed Phil Rodgers 13 shots back.

Tom Weiskopf matched Palmer's aggregate of 276 when the Open returned to Troon in 1973. Locked in battle with Johnny Miller in the third and fourth rounds and with Nicklaus making one of his memorable "charges" in the last round, Weiskopf, who had opening rounds of 68 and 67, held on to win. Tom Watson added a fourth of five Open Championships at the height of his illustrious career in 1982—the same year he won the U.S. Open. Arnold Palmer was made an honorary member of Royal Troon Golf Club that year.

Five Troon Opens in a row have been won by Americans. Following Watson was Mark Calcavecchia in 1989, who beat Greg Norman in a play-off. Justin Leonard was the last in 1997 before Royal Troon hosted the Open again in 2004 for the eighth time over a period spanning 80 years.

ROYAL TROON **RIGHT**: TWO VIEWS OF THE 10TH HOLE, THE BLIND TEE SHOT AND THE APPROACH TO THE GREEN. **OPPOSITE**: THE 18TH GREEN AND CLUBHOUSE.

LOOKING BACK THROUGH THE 1ST GREEN AND FAIRWAY TO THE CLUBHOUSE, WHICH ENJOYS PANORAMIC VIEWS OVER THE COURSE AND ACROSS THE SEA TO THE ISLAND OF ARRAN.

Western Gailes & Glasgow Gailes

ontinuing up the West Coast toward Glasgow are a group of three prime links in Western Gailes, Glasgow Gailes and the new Dundonald course skirting the old Glasgow to Ayr railway line. When Glasgow Golf Club was reconstituted in 1870 (records are vague before this) the members played in the city. From the South Side Park they moved to the more open quarters at Alexandra Park in the East End. This ground had a cold clay soil, long coarse grass, no sand hazards, and became bogged down in the winter months. Thus a piece of more traditional links ground was sought where members could jump off a train and play by the seaside at any time of the year!

Willie Park Jr. laid out the course next to the Gailes railway station in

WESTERN GAILES THE 7TH TEE TO GREEN PAR 3. THE GREEN IS PROTECTED BY NUMEROUS POT BUNKERS AND CLASSICAL DUNE LAND MAKING IT BOTH A GOLFING CHALLENGE AND VISUAL FEAST.

WESTERN GAILES THE 8TH IS A SLIGHT DOG-LEG RIGHT AND IS A CHALLENGE BOTH FROM THE TEE AND FOR THE APPROACH SHOT. DISTANCE AND ACCURACY ARE AN ISSUE AS BUNKERS LINE THE LEFT SIDE OF THE FAIRWAY WITH LONG GRASSES AND THE BEACH TO THE RIGHT.

1892 for the club and it was an instant success. So much so that a group of 11 enthusiasts got together after looking at an equally good stretch next door to the Glasgow Gailes course on the south side, and managed to acquire a lease from the Duke of Portland (same owner of the land at Troon) and thus the Western Gailes club was formed in 1897. It was very much a hands-on, do-it-yourself job, with no funding for an established, course architect or any facility even for changing, apart from in the green keepers hut. The course was vulnerable to flooding from high tides and storms, it being so exposed. Despite all the initial problems a life membership was offered at £5 in 1901 and enough interest and, more importantly at the time, money, was generated to build a clubhouse. Harry Vardon,

after winning the Open at Prestwick in 1903, gave the club a boost by playing the course in competition and setting an impressive course record of 68, while watched by large crowds. To keep up and improve the maintenance of Western Gailes, what had become old and traditional methods were adopted, such as marram and bent grasses for the unstable and shifting sand-duned areas to knit together and stop erosion. The original 600 founding members were well rewarded for their vision and dogged perseverance in establishing, and in 1920 buying, the linksland that was eventually to become an Open Championship qualifying course. Both the British Senior and Boys Amateur Championships have been played over the links, along with the PGA Championship and the Curtis Cup.

WESTERN GAILES   THE 8TH GREEN IS PROTECTED ALONG THE FRONT BY THE, ALMOST OBLIGATORY, BURN AND BUNKERS.

Scottish Golf Links

DUNDONALD COURSE

As if following the move of Glasgow Golf Club over 100 years earlier, Loch Lomond Golf Club, in a magnificent backdrop of Scottish hill and loch, acquired the former Southern Gailes links as an alternative type of course and setting for its members and guests. Within an hour's drive down to the southwest coast to Ayrshire, the new course shares the same breathtaking views across the Firth of Clyde to the Isle of Arran as that of the established "Gailes."

"Dundonald" was appropriately named after a fort up on the hill behind the course which dates back to 500 B.C. At different times during the centuries, three castles have succeeded the original structure. In the early 1900s there had been a course named Dundonald, which, like Turnberry, was "arrested" during the Second World War and converted into a military camp. Unlike the Turnberry courses and their successful appeal for compensation from the government to restructure, this one just slipped quietly away!

Now 7,300 yards from the championship tees, Dundonald has already made its mark as a premier course. In the way that Kingsbarns has made such an impact with the quality of its new links on the east coast, Kyle Phillips was called in to do "the same again" (like ordering a whisky) on the west coast. Although an American course architect, he had an empathy, a true feel and love of linksland, evident in his Kingsbarns layout. Opened prior to the Troon Open Championship in 2004, Dundonald has added to the impressive, closely-linked parade of courses on the Ayrshire coast.

DUNDONALD **OPPOSITE**: THE EARLY MORNING LIGHT VIVIDLY HIGHLIGHTS THE GORSE IN THIS VIEW FROM THE 4TH TEE TOWARDS THE GREEN. **ABOVE**: LOOKING BACK THOUGH THE 6TH GREEN TOWARDS THE TEE. IN THE DISTANCE THE FLAGS OF THE 8TH AND 13TH GREENS HANG MOTIONLESS IN THE LATE AFTERNOON WINTER AIR. **BELOW**: THE APPROACH TO THE 8TH GREEN.

DUNDONALD **ABOVE**: LONG GRASSES FRAME THE 17TH GREEN AND, IN THE DISTANCE, THE MOST CHALLENGING 12TH GREEN. **RIGHT**: THE GORSE IN BLOOM DURING THE LATE SPRING ADDS A SPLASH OF COLOUR TO THE 9TH AND 18TH GREENS. **OPPOSITE**: LOCH LOMOND GOLF COURSE 5TH TEE TO GREEN PAR 3.

It is inevitable that I view the merits of a golf course by the opportunities it offers for producing good photographs. The opportunity for the sun to cast shadows over undulating terrain, the natural textures, shapes and colours of long grasses, gorse, heather and trees. All of these features add atmosphere and beauty to the photographer's eye, but are also an integral part of the design. I have always found that if a course photographs well then it is fair to assume that it will be equally rewarding and challenging for the golfer, and vice versa.

Dundonald is a new course designed by Kyle Phillips which, although not having the benefit of seas not crashing on bordering shores, has been a joy to photograph. It possesses all of the beauty and challenge to be expected of a great Scottish links course, but it is also recognised, in the editorial world, as a course of exceptional quality and possible venue for the Scottish Open.

I mention all of this at this point because I find it reassuring to see new courses (Kingsbarns and Dundonald), from the east and west coasts, that still capture the magic of our much older links courses.

This part of the journey is a momentary diversion away from links courses and into the heartland of a rugged and inspiring Scotland. Glimpses of the ever changing face of Loch Lomond as the route moves north and then, after turning west, the road leads into Glen Croe, meandering upwards under towering hills. Finally, in the blink of an eye, it bursts free from the confines of the inland countryside, out to the wide expanse of Loch Fyne. The coast of this sea loch is dotted with picturesque towns and villages each waiting to be explored. I find this to be amongst the most spectacular and beautiful scenery in Scotland. Here, more than anywhere else, I make time to stop and enjoy all that surrounds me, a moment of tranquillity and a pause for quiet thought.

Scottish Golf Links

OPPOSITE: BEYOND THE WEATHER WORN COASTLINE, ACROSS THE BAY, MACHRIHANISH NESTLES UNDER THE DISTANT HILL. **ABOVE**: THE TOWN OF INVERARY, ON THE DISTANT BANK OF LOCH FYNE, IS PART OF THE ROUTE TO MACHRIHANISH. **RIGHT**: BARREN PEAKS THAT SURROUND THE JOURNEY THROUGH THE HILLS AND GLENS.

The Islands

The islands, so prominent from the west coast links, have a surprising amount of courses of their own worth visiting. On the Isle of Arran alone there are seven, including Shiskine—a quirky Tom Morris 12-hole layout from around 1891. Even the remote Hebridean Islands had four recognised courses in the 1890s.

MACHRIE

On the Island of Islay, famous for its peaty malt whiskies, a links course was laid out by Willie Campbell, a prominent professional, after a club was formed in 1890. Campbell joined the exodus of Scots pros to the States and was runner-up in the first, but unofficial, U.S. Open in 1893. After visiting the island and the proposed site along an impressive duned area by the golden sands of Laggan Bay, Campbell reported to the Islay Golf Club, "It is the best ground for a golf course that I have ever had the pleasure of viewing. Sir, I can say that for very little money, it will become one of the best courses in Scotland as it will need very little more than cutting the putting greens and making a bridge here and there. If this was done you could play golf the next day." It was another example of utilising prime golfing real estate in the 1890s!

A challenge match was set up between Campbell and Willie Fernie, the 1883 Open Champion and professional at Troon, to open the Machrie course in 1891, which was well publicised on the mainland. Campbell won the substantial purse and the course immediately attracted attention to itself despite the difficulty in getting to the island. In 1901 just after the Muirfield Open, the Triumvirate of Vardon, Taylor, and Braid and most of the top professionals made the arduous journey across to Islay to play in a match play tournament at the Machrie to compete for a £100 prize. James Braid was narrowly beaten by J.H.Taylor in the final when it was said that a rabbits' dropping deflected his ball from the last hole when trying to save the match!

At that time it was considered the longest and most difficult course to score on, but has since become more hospitable with improvements to its general condition in the 1970s. It is still a real test of links golf and well worth a visit if you are inclined to sample the many malts distilled on the way to the Machrie. (They say that the air is 30% proof on the island!)

ONE FINAL DIVERSION, BY FERRY OR AIR, ACROSS TO THE ISLAY GOLF COURSE AT THE MACHRIE HOTEL ON THE ISLAND OF ISLAY. THIS COURSE PLAYS AMONGST, OVER AND AROUND SOME MOST IMPRESSIVE SAND DUNES, IN FACT IT IS PROTECTED SO WELL BY NATURAL TERRAIN THAT IT ONLY HAS NINE BUNKERS.
LEFT: THE 1ST GREEN IS A BLIND APPROACH SHOT THAT MUST CLEAR THE BUNKER.
BELOW: THE COURSE ENJOYS COUNTLESS BLIND SHOTS AND THE 17TH IS A PAR 4 THAT REQUIRES A COMPLETELY BLIND SHOT OVER THE DUNE TO A GREEN WHICH, NOT SURPRISINGLY, HAS NO BUNKERS.

MACHRIHANISH An aerial view of this impressive links course with the 7th green and fairway to the right and the 12th to the left.

MACHRIHANISH

It's a lyrical way to end this photographer's journey by slowly winding round Loch Lomond and driving down through spectacular scenery to the south tip of the Mull of Kintyre and Campbeltown. There lies Machrihanish, a mystical place in the world of golf.

On Monday, March the twentieth in 1876, the first sod of the newly formed Kintyre Golf Club was cut and a now-celebrated "homemade" 10-hole course was born. The keeper of the Prestwick green, Charlie Hunter, was called over to see what they'd done and added his touch and an extra two holes. Three years later Tom Morris was brought across from St. Andrews and with additional ground created a full 18-hole course. "Created" is the wrong word, for Old Tom was quick to announce that "providence assuredly saw this part of the country as a special earthly Paradise designed by the Almighty for playing golf." The Golfing Annual 20 years later said, "The links of Machrihanish are universally admitted by those who have played over them to be the finest of all." A bold statement to make when all the major links courses were well established apart from Turnberry. It was at a time when the journey was likened to a pilgrimage of old, across sea, moor, and mountain! The proprietors of the Argyll and White Hart Hotels in Cambeltown ran two "wagonettes" a week to and from the links five miles down the road for golfing visitors during the summer months, as well as one in the winter months.

With the reputation of the Machrihanish links growing rapidly, the one local hotel, Pans, added considerable additions to its sleepy, mystical location and by 1896, had 80 rooms, a billiard room, tennis courts, and conveyances attending the arrival and departure of the steamers at Cambeltown. Since then, J.H.Taylor had a hand in 1914 in protecting the almost sacred image of the links, as did Sir Guy Campbell after Coastal Command and the Fleet Air Arm demanded facilities and priority tee times during the Second World War!…heartfelt thanks to all the protectors of what has become a truly unique experience at Machrihanish on the Scottish Links Trail.

MACHRIHANISH THE 1ST TEE OFFERS A DAUNTING OPENING SHOT A LITTLE BETTER EXPLAINED BY THE AERIAL PICTURE.

Because of a decision to change the clubhouse position and original course design many years ago, the rhythm of the course is now similar to the reverse of a great concert, the crescendo is performed first. The beginning 8 holes are some of the best in all of links golf, both from a strategic and scenic standpoint. The physical and visual impact of a now closed, military air base makes it difficult to fully appreciate the equally strong architecture that continues through holes 9–14. However, both the natural landscape, as well as the quality of the architecture begins diminish from 15 to 18, leaving a hollow feeling at the finish.

Part of the lore of Machrihanish is the long journey through some of the finest landscape in the world. A right turn at Campbeltown and just a few more miles up the road awaits Machrinhanish, as far removed from the hurried pace of the 21st century as one can get.

Machrihanish #3

The 3rd is one of the best blind driving holes I have ever played. The tee shot plays across the back of the 16th green and over the horizon towards the sea. A wide fairway, that rewards a ball played down the right center, waits out of view. Even though the approach is not long, a dune guards the front left pin and will send shots that are just slightly short scooting to the back of the deep green, leaving long return putts. The strong support on the right side of the green surface can be equally challenging for drives left to the right, particularly when the pin favours the right portion of the green.

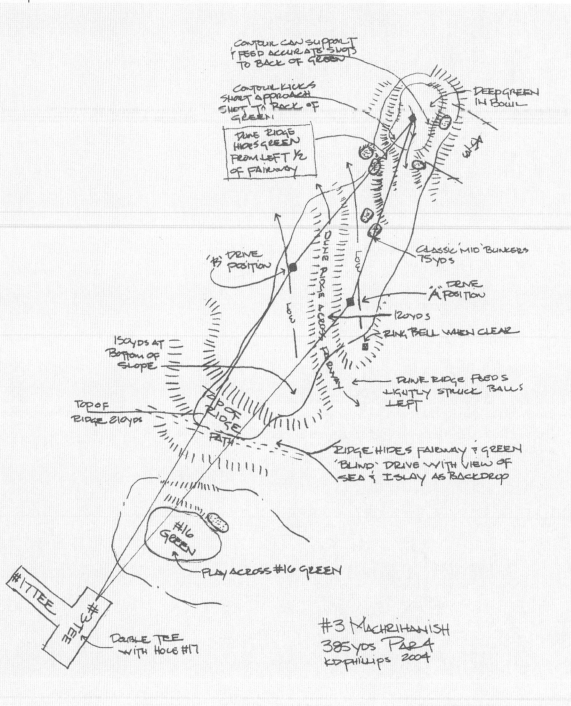

ABOVE: ANY BLIND DRIVE CAN BE UNSETTLING BUT THE 3RD AT MACHRIHANISH, OVER THE 16TH GREEN, TAKES IT A LITTLE BIT FURTHER.

BELOW: THE APPROACH TO THE GREEN, SEEMINGLY RINGED BY BUNKERS.

MACHRIHANISH HAS A MOST UNUSUAL ATMOSPHERE, ALMOST A FEELING OF DETACHMENT FROM REALITY, MOST APPARENT FROM THE 3RD TO THE 9TH HOLES. I SUSPECT THIS IS IN PART DUE TO THE TERRAIN. EACH HOLE SEEMS TO STAND ALONE, VIRTUALLY HIDDEN FROM OTHERS BY GRASS COVERED SAND DUNES, WITH ONLY THE OCCASIONAL CRY OF SUCCESS OR FAILURE CARRIED ON THE WIND TO INDICATE THE PRESENCE OF OTHER GOLFERS. **ABOVE**: LOOKING BACK THROUGH THE 4TH GREEN TO THE TEE AND TOWN BEYOND. **OPPOSITE, LEFT**: LOOKING BACK THROUGH THE 5TH GREEN WITH A DEEP GULLY TO THE FRONT LEFT AND RIGHT. **OPPOSITE, RIGHT**: THE 6TH TEE TO GREEN. THIS IS A SHORT PAR FOUR, JUST 300 YARDS BUT THE SEMI-BLIND TEE SHOT POSES THE UNCERTAINTY OF UNKNOWN DANGER.

244   Scottish Golf Links

MACHRIHANISH **OPPOSITE**: THE VIEW FROM THE 8TH TEE TO THE MARKER POST WITH THE GREEN PERCHED UP ON THE TOP LEFT IS SO TYPICAL OF THIS SECTION OF HOLES. **BELOW**: THE 10TH HOLE, A DOG-LEG LEFT PAR 5, PLAYS BACK TOWARDS THE TOWN. IT HERALDS THE START OF THE SECTION OF HOLES THAT PLAYS AROUND THE OUTER EDGE OF THE MAJOR DUNE LAND BUT CONTINUES TO OFFER THE CHALLENGE OF UNDULATING FAIRWAYS LEADING TO GREENS SET BACK INTO NATURAL LINKS LAND. **RIGHT**: THE APPROACH UP TO THE ELEVATED 12TH GREEN.

AT THE END OF THE DAY THE WIND DROPS AND THE SUN CASTS ITS FINAL BLAZE OF COLOUR OVER THE 18TH GREEN AT MACHRIHANISH. THIS, MORE THAN ANY OTHER, IS A SPECIAL TIME, THE GOLFERS ARE GONE, THE BIRDS ARE RESTING AND ABSOLUTE PEACE SETTLES OVER THE COURSE WITH THE GATHERING DARKNESS.

Fireworks heralded the 250th Anniversary of The Royal and Ancient at the end of a memorable evening for invited guests of all the St. Andrews golf clubs. In the year 2004 at the end of May, in the biggest two story marquee ever constructed in Scotland, eleven hundred and sixty people sat down to dine. Their host was the R&A captain for the year, H.R.H. The Duke of York, who presided over another three grand occasions under canvas during that week, commemorating the club's rich and colourful past. The original twenty-two nobles and gentlemen from the kingdom of Fife met to play in their first Spring Meeting of 1754, and later toast the game of golf in Bailie Glass's hostelry. They would surely never have imagined, in such modest surroundings, how the game would grow and the heather bloom all around the royal and ancient golf links of Scotland.